HOW TO FIX YOUR CREDIT:

RAISING YOUR CREDIT SCORE FROM POOR TO EXCELLENT

TABLE OF CONTENTS

Introduction

Chapter One Understanding the Basics

Chapter Two Maximizing your Credit Score

Chapter Three What to Know about Credit Reporting Agencies

Chapter Four The Relationship between Debts and Credit

Chapter Five Fifteen Credit Score Myths to Unlearn

Chapter Six Credit Errors and Disputes

Chapter Seven Credit Counselling: Do you Really Need One?

Chapter Eight The Truths about Bankruptcy

Chapter Nine Simple Strategies to Fix your Credit

Conclusion Mistakes to Avoid During Credit Repair

Copyright 2019 by Ruben Hanson

All rights reserved. This book or parts thereof may not be reproduced in any form, stored in any retrieval system, or transmitted in any form by any means—electronic, mechanical, photocopy, recording, or otherwise—without prior written permission of the publisher, except as provided by United States of America copyright law.

All rights reserved. No portion of this book may be reproduced in any form without permission from the publisher, except as permitted by U.S. copyright law.

Introduction

Logan Miller

Denver, Colorado. Feb 2011

"I'm afraid this is a rather difficult situation, Mr. Miller. I understand your plight quite alright, but as much as I would like to help you, my hands are tied. It is our strict principle here at The Bank of Denver never to give out loans in excess of $5000 to individuals with a credit score less than 640, and to think that your account here with us is only a step away from dormancy. You might have to check elsewhere please."

Logan found it difficult to stay focused on the words of the bank manager after it became evident that this was another dead end. A copy of his credit report was right there on the desk between him and the manager, bearing the testimony of his financial challenges, and reminding him that he just might not make it out of this one. As his eyes rested on the piece of art hanging on the wall behind the bank manager, his mind wandered back to all his previous attempts and failures at securing a loan — what would have been his fifth loan in the past twelve months. He had tried the Wealth Legacy Institute, MountainView Financial Solution and E* Trade as well as banks such as the Wells Fargo Bank, and the Bank of America. He had also tried banks situated outside Denver for a loan as little as $5000. *Just $5000,* he thought. But none agreed to offer him even less than that. It was always *Your credit score is too bad* and another door would be slammed in his face! A friend had suggested The Bank of Denver saying they were currently running a special loan package for businesspersons.

Mr. Miller? Are you there?

As the words of the manager intruded on his thoughts and brought him back to the present, he was surprised at himself that he had been so lost in thought and suddenly began to feel sweat balls forming on his forehead. He made a final weak effort.

Erh... You mean there's really no chance whatsoever? He asked.

I'm afraid none, Mr. Miller

Alright, I'll leave then.

With hands rendered feeble by grief, he slowly gathered his papers and rose to go, and the thoughts flooded back into his mind unhindered with as much force as liquid from a damaged water pipe, bringing back to his memory for the umpteenth time how his woes had all started about two years ago when he had incurred a bad debt in his estate management business. For the first time since he started about five years before, he fell into the hands of fraudsters, and rather too cheaply. Now that he thought about it again, he wondered how he did not think that $100,000 was too low for the string of apartments he had been shown. Hoping to make nothing less than 500% returns over the course of ten years, he had rallied around and gathered the funds from a few trusted associates, and that single decision was the beginning of the end of his career. Perhaps his situation would not have been so bad if he had paid proper attention to his credit records all along. The reality dawned when he discovered that he had a score less than 450, which had continued to decrease as he jumped from one small debt to another in a bid to salvage what was left of his career. As if the world was in strong connivance against him, he had suffered multiple blows outside his career as well. Only three weeks earlier, he had been notified of the expiration of his rent in six weeks' time. He had barely two weeks left to sort out the rent or would be ejected from a home where he had lived for four years. He sighed and thought again of his credit score. If only it wasn't so bad.

*****

Like our friend, Logan Miller, there are tons of individuals looking for a job, business persons in need of loans, employees in search of greener pastures, individuals looking to rent a suitable apartment, and many other such categories of persons who have been deprived opportunities that could have improved their career and/or personal lives solely because such privileges require a good credit history. As the world continues to evolve in its practices, virtually every domain of life requires a dependable means of safety and security, especially when financial transactions are involved. The mortgage firm wants to be assured you can repay your loan in due time; the employer needs to be sure you wouldn't be a financial liability if you are employed, as well as your ability to manage both personal and company funds; the landlord or property manager wants to be convinced that you wouldn't have a difficulty meeting up with the required rent in due time; the insurance company wants to know if you can keep up with your premium after three or more years, and the financial institution needs an assurance of your tendency to repay your loan duly, among many other situations.

You see, it is almost impossible in the modern world to pass through an organization without being asked for your credit report. Sadly, many people have been caught on the wrong side of this trend for several reasons including reckless credit management, the incurrence of bad debts and failure to repay, late payment of bills, and so on. With this book in your hand, it is safe to assume that you are either new to the idea of credit score and would like to learn how to get a favorable one or you are looking to learn how to fix your already damaged credit. Whichever the situation is with you, you are in the right direction. Fixing your credit does not require magic or a miracle. Getting a good credit score is a product of very little progressive acts that take place over a period of time. However, I understand how dire and quickly you would like to fix your credit if you fall into the latter category. Hence, I provide in this book practical easy DIY strategies that can boost your credit score to at least 700 in a matter of weeks. In the same vein, if you are just about to set out on building your credit score, you will find these strategies indispensable. You do not have to wait till you need a loan or till you're asked by an employer to bring your report before taking your credit score seriously. The best time is now! To help you understand the ideas and processes suggested in this book, I will first walk you through the most fundamental basics about credit, credit report, credit score indices, the benefits of having a good credit score as well as the downside of having a low credit score, among many other key factors to know. It is a quick journey to building and boosting your financial experience. Brace up!

What is Credit? What is a Credit Score?

Broadly speaking, credit refers to the procurement of an item or service with an agreement to pay at a later time. In most advanced societies, this is often done with credit cards. Little goods and services may be purchased on credit because the buyer is not with physical cash at the moment to pay for the given services but with the understanding that the payment will be made at a future time. In more serious cases, credit is the worthiness of an individual or firm to receive funds from another individual or organization with the mutual understanding to pay back in the future with certain terms and conditions as agreed. This worthiness to receive funds and pay later is based on an individual's or organization's credit history and earlier transactions. To put it most simply, for you to be considered for a loan or any other financial benefit, you must have had a record of smooth transactions, refunds, and payment of bills, among others, to qualify you. It is only logical to expect that if you have been able to pay a previous loan, you should be capable of paying back the present one in due time. However, do not be conditioned to believe from my illustrations so far that credit involves loans only. As a matter of fact, it means much more which I will dwell so much on later in this book.

This creditworthiness is measured in solid figures using several scoring systems, popular among which are Vantage 3.0 and FICO. Over time, the Fair Isaac Corporation score has been adopted in many societies. An individual's or organization's FICO score is generated using statistics derived from the calculation of your payment patterns, loan repayment, the amount of your debts, the number of credit cards you own and several other factors. Ratings may range from 300, which is considered low to about 850, which is considered high. A high credit score implies that you have an excellent credit history and can repay all your loans in due time. On the other hand, a low credit score implies the opposite. It is such information concerning your financial history that the credit bureaus send to your lenders, employers or landlord as the case may be to help them make a decision concerning your request. An important fact to bear in mind is that your credit score might vary depending on the area of focus of the organization requesting it. For instance, your FICO score for an insurance company might differ significantly from a department store or a mortgage bank. The only way to develop a great credit score that will serve multiple purposes and organizations is to undertake careful strategies, as will be suggested in this book, to build a thorough credit history. Although a credit score is represented in simple three figures, it wields a lot of significance on an individual's career and finance, and by extension, every other sector of one's life that relies on finance. The same applies to organizations and firms. Your credit score can make or mar you greatly, and this explains why it should be given sufficient attention.

In a bid to develop their credit record, businesspersons, individuals and firms concentrate more on what they think will improve their creditworthiness in neglect of what they should not do to maintain their credit. In fact, it would interest you to learn that some persons are not aware of the don'ts of financial transactions if you must maintain good credit. As a result of this ignorant neglect, many good credits have turned gross in no time. If this resonates with you, you are one of the categories of persons this book is addressed to. In the same vein, if you are just looking to start up your credit history anew, you will find the potholes to avoid as well as the active steps to take to help you garner as much as a credit score of over 700 in a few weeks. The ideas suggested here are easy, practical and productive for efficient speedy credit repair. If you are ready, I'm all set. Let's ride!

CHAPTER ONE

UNDERSTANDING THE BASICS

What is Credit?

Credit is a technical name that you want to put in your head every moment you step into the business world. Maybe much bigger than a name, a vital instrument that can give life to your business, as much as your investment itself. It is the first alternative that crosses the mind of every businessman when there isn't enough cash to keep the business running and you are pretty sure nobody is investing sometime soon. Credit can be your business's lifeline, and that extra touch you need to splash on your business to make it flourish. I have to say though, it is not a great idea to start a business with it, and that's because, in some cases, such businesses don't get far. You reel in debts and at the end, fold up the company. So, you should start with your capital and build with credits, taking calculated risks.

I will begin by telling you what credit is exactly. Credit is the general name for every good or service you get from the owners for a fixed period, with the mutual agreement that you're paying them back sometime later. It is what you get when you walk into a firm and try to convince them to supply you some of their services, assuring you'd clear the bills before a fixed time, or in an agreed method. At other times, you do not even take services or goods on credit, you get soft loans with a promise to pay back. By that, I'm talking about money and that's the most popular credit.

Practically, you can get credits from friends (documented of course), from business partners, merchants and as you would guess, banks and other financial institutions. There are professional creditors or lenders around too; a set of businessmen who are ready to offer you services, goods or money on loan any second you need some. They are, in fact, the richest sources of *Credit*. You can walk into their office and get out the *Credit* you need from them any second. Though, in most cases, this doesn't always work that way. Many even find it the most difficult option. Why? Empirical research proves that only 21% of people who apply for loans eventually get as much as they need in a hand-in hand-deal. The staggering percentage of those left do not get enough in most cases, and the few times some do, they get horrible deals that force them to surrender well over half of their profits to the hands of the lenders. It is why many people think lenders are dreadful humans you should avoid when you can.

But is that always true? Of course not. They are businessmen all right, but they didn't come to the market to make sure their clients, the other businesses who lend from them, crumble. After all, you can't come for their credits if you have got no trade to fund in the first place, and they get their little interests, and their wealth from the profit you turnover. So, you see they gain nothing from crushing other businesses, there's just something about 79% aren't doing right when applying for credit. What could be that be? You will read every one of them in the next lines, and first, we will begin by mentioning the various kinds of credits.

Types of Credit

There is an endless list of the kinds of credit you can get, depends on whom you ask. The list gets wider if you are considering financial credit of some sort. The simplest of them are those loans you get from friends or families, usually backed with promissory notes. Then, there are formal, larger and bigger ones like credit cards, auto loans, mortgage, bank loans, overdrafts, mortgages, personal loans, purchase loans, schooling loans and a lot of other loans you didn't know exist. You can't apply for every one of them every time. A lot of consideration sets in when you need to get one, and they determine whom you turn to at those times.

You may turn to your bank for automobile loans, your friends for business loans and so forth. But it will be pretty hard to file out all the kind of loans possible and whom you turn to each time you need them. Some forms of credits are recognized in some communities and not in others. Besides, there are policies guiding them and some stand to be modified, eradicated or established, all dependent on government policies. This book is set to be your guide forever, so rather than list all those credits, the varieties of credit would be grouped into two major categories which you can always group the others into. They are:

a. **The Open-End Credit**: These are simple forms of credits that can be taken at any time. Usually, a credit card company gives such a loan by issuing a credit card. It is quite possible to buy products while the charges are drawn on the credit company, and they look forward to being paid when the month ends. In some cases, you don't have to complete the total credit drawn in the month at once, they can be paid consistently over time. It is what you'd hear people call *Revolving credit*. Practical examples are home equity loans, home equity lines of credit (HELOC), service credits and of course Credit Cards (which can be used for daily expenses, wears, transportation, etc.) are all examples of cases like this.

b. **The Close-End Credit**: Credits like these are drawn to finance a specific purpose within an agreed period. They are the type you draw on auto loans, mortgage, student loans, et cetera. The payment method, duration, and all related items are agreed upon from the start. It is dangerous not to meet such agreed terms because you risk losing your collaterals to the lending company. They are often called *installment credits*. Every other credit can be grouped into one of these.

Now, you can easily group the form of credit you'd like to draw. You should at the same time understand possible factors that can influence the success or failure of your loan application all discussed in the next chapter.

What is your credit score?

Your credit score is a form of the previous score that can predict your chances of returning your proposed client to the lender if they eventually lend you. You can consider the credit score a sort of factual report from your previous employer to your next employer, presenting details of how committed you were at your formal job. But this time, it isn't on employment, it presents a statistical analysis of your previous loans, the agreed rules, the payment pattern and how well you adhere to every one of them. There are different ways of ranking each loan, however, they can all be compiled and analyzed by analyzing companies like FICO.

By FICO's guides, the highest total credit score anyone can ever get is 999. And 850 and above are considered awesome scores. Before you can make such scores, you must be the type who has great credit refunding records. You have to pay up your loans pretty quick and have impressive business transactions. You are considered very reliable too. Most lending companies would be more than willing to offer credits to anyone who belongs to this class.

Strangely, two different business magazines report that only 7% of debtors fit into that category in most cases. The remaining entrepreneurs never made it to that stage. The 850 and above class of people can't ever have problems obtaining credits from anyone. They get all the loans they need and play by the rules as strictly as possible. That's unlike anyone who is below 600. Their credit card score is considered pretty low, and creditors don't think they are reliable. So, convincing lending firms or credit unions for a big loan might be pretty hard for them, and they often end up not getting what they want. This is why you must pay earnest attention to how you pay your loans. The average credit score is "650 to 720" while 720-850 stands a better chance.

Anyone whose credit score doesn't make one of these lists may find it hellish to secure fair close-end loans. And that's why you should keep your eyes on the scores. If you are not sure how to calculate your credit score, you may contact any of Equifax, TransUnion or Experian for your free copy. They usually send that in a detailed credit report. By the way, that's once or twice a year. So, I am going to teach you how to do it yourself in some of the next lines.

What is your Credit Report?

Have you heard "credit report" and you cannot help guessing it is? You are likely right; the meaning is what could have crossed your mind the first time you try to explain it to yourself. A credit report is a standard breakdown of your financial record. That's where you find details of your interaction with previous lending companies. Your current position and your chances of getting new credits, in other words, your credit score.

What does a credit report contain? Usually, you would find four sections in your credit report. The first section details your personal information that will necessarily include your name, social security number and such business-related information. When you open the next section, which is called *Trade Lines*, you will find a "bit by bit" analysis of your financial interaction, credit and as you would guess, credit statistics. The third section displays the public judgments you and your company have received, especially on financial issues and related cases, but mainly on finances. The last section details the group of people who have legal rights to request your credit information and have requested your credit report for pertinent business consideration. Usually, nobody has a right to your credit information, but the moment you are involved in, or request to get involved in credit transactions with a firm, they have a right to understand your financial state and may, with your consent, request for your credit report.

Now you understand that your credit report is a vital document you should have around you always, consulting it now and then and noting the progress in it. It can determine a lot, from your chances of getting loans, to investing and such financial activities. If you do not have a copy of these, you may contact any of the firms mentioned on credit scores for your copy.

Credit History: Going Back in Time

It is interesting to tell you that much beyond the general tales you hear about credits, the idea of credit is one of the oldest activities in history. You know, modern investors like to make us think they did everything. Right, the idea of credit cards started in the 20th century among other things, but the original picture of credit (loan) must have begun at least 5,000 years ago. Notable scholars like Jeff D. believe the Sumerians (the oldest community known to have lived on earth) have at some point offered credits to each other, lending agricultural produce for consumption, with the hope of paying back soon. This history traces it down to the Babylonians, Syrians, and the different development stages in Europe.

Another interesting fact is that credit reporting was first started by a group of tailors. They suspected some of their clients owe others, and would likely owe them so they gathered to submit and examine financial reports of each of their clients. This was in England, 1803, before 1826 when The Manchester Guardian Society began to publish the names of anyone who owes others and refused to pay every month. Tracking companies' creditworthiness began with the Mercantile Agency in New York, before the Retail Credit Company, a company now known as Equifax today was established in 1899 to research into and publish the list of creditworthy companies in New York. Afterward, several developments have been recorded, including Frank

McNamara's introduction of credit cards in 1950. To date, momentums are witnessed in the credit industry, you may add yours sometime.

Already, you have a good idea of what credit card, card report, and credit can do to your business. You also know what it means to have a high or low credit scores on your report. You will have little worries if you make high scores in your credit report. But if you don't, you will likely wonder, *is this how things are going to stay? Can I ever up this thing to a better score?* The answer is yes, you can. If you are wondering how to keep up your high scores too, you will learn that and how to spruce up your scores in the next pages.

Chapter Summary

This chapter launches into the exposition of the concepts of credit and credit fixing or credit repair in a bid to give you an understanding of the basics you need before you can increase it from poor to excellent.

CHAPTER TWO

MAXIMIZING YOUR CREDIT SCORE

Maximizing your credit scores is something you must make a mission whether or not you are already into the business. That's how you can stand a better chance of bigger funds, bigger support, and a bigger business the next time you need to call for money.

Why Raise Your Credit Score?

Here are the top reasons you must take raising your credit score seriously:

a. **Lower Interest Rates**: Do you remember I mentioned this in the last chapter? There are very high chances that investors do not want to offer you a loan when you have a poor credit score. In the circumstances that they do, you should expect perilous interest rates, the type that could make you want to shut your company because you almost gained nothing. A lot of times, these companies set their policies that way. A notorious credit company in some western parts of the United States, for the whole of 2018 charges 35% interest for credit withdrawn on very low credit scores and only 4% for high credit scores. So, you see, you need to upgrade to high scores. They are sure they are getting their funds, their profits, and lending it off to someone else in a short while, and they would heel up all you requested without troubles.

b. **Higher Chances of More Loans**: This is a very practical situation. Imagine you have a friend who runs down to your office to lend some cash once in a while, he would always return a few hours after, with your money and the agreed interest. Would you ever have any worry lending him again when he shows up the 100th time? I bet you won't. It's just how these firms work too. Even if you approach a credit firm you haven't ever got a loan from, they can tell from your credit report and credit scores whether or not you are the type who honors your deals. Already, their calculations are on how reliable and how soon their monies will be refunded. So, whether you want a bigger, smaller, or the same range of credit, you stand a higher chance with a high credit score.

c. **No Firm Gets a Chance to Harass you**: If you have a poor credit score, you are likely indebted to some firms over a long time. Whether you want it or not, that firm will ring you now and then, stalk you in and out of your work and home, keep their eyes on your bank account, collateral, send you heartbreaking emails and cause you to be unhappy. Your best way out of a case like that, or to even avoid is to pay quickly and hit an attractive credit score.

d. **Stand a Chance of Bigger Loans**: This comes with a high and stable credit score too. Everyone thinks they can stake a chance on you if you have got great credit records and you suddenly turn up, requesting a credit larger than what you've had. Credit is in steps, you know. Nobody issues out billions at the first approach, you have got to build a long and impressive credit record on slightly lower credits before you stand a chance of higher loans.

e. **You Get a Lower Insurance Rate**: This is something most people don't know. If you run on a very low credit score and you think your insurance premiums are pretty high, put it in mind that your charges are that high because you are on a low credit rate. A high credit score means you move pretty well on your auto loans or mortgage, and you don't have so much to pay again. Perhaps you even have it all cleared. You are bound to have a cheap and cheerful insurance premium then. If you'd like to confirm how right that is, get a much better credit score and compare the prices.

f. **The Rare Need for Sureties**: With impressive financial records, most credit firms would not stand intent on seeing your sureties before offering your loans. You won't find it hard to get sureties too anyway because your records speak for you. The opposite story goes for anyone on low credit scores. Despite providing all that is needed, co-signatories or sureties are always required. So, once you promote to high scores, you know how easy things can be for you.

g. **You can Achieve the Goals of your Life Easily**: No matter how simple your job is, you can get the car, house, education and every goal of your dreams if you keep an amazing record. You may have held records of smaller credits, but many would take a chance on you considering your immaculate record. And there it is: your dreams falling into place one after the other!

h. **Keep your Life and Business Moving**: You want to keep a happy and free human life. You want to keep your business flourishing with larger credits and bigger profits. These are the reasons you must, as a matter of necessity, keep a great credit record. You don't want to start hide-and-find games with everyone, faking your death or committing suicide because the troubles of your crediting firms are getting too intense. Therefore, you must do all you can to make sure you meet the clauses agreed in your credit contract.

These are some of the reasons you should fix your credit score to the highest you can, there are a few other reasons which you may even discover yourself. Don't you think you should work on maximizing your credit scores as much as you can now? I know you do, but you do not know how. Stay tuned, and you will discover soon. In the subsequent paragraphs, I will walk you through the factors you didn't know could influence your efforts at building a great credit score.

Factors That Reduce Your Credit Score

Just before we mention how to box up your credit scores. Let's see, what are the stats that can knock life out of your credit cards?

a. **Payment History**: This is the peak and most important of it all. Your potential creditors are interested in your payment history. How consistent you were while paying the other loans, how you stuck to the agreed regulations and how many credits you have committed yourself to and paid as per the regulations. This can help them foretell how you would pay their credits. If you have an average overall credit score or moved fairly above average, you may still have a tough time convincing the crediting firm if you have a poor payment history. Because, literarily, what they can read from your payment history (which matters most to them) is that you have taken various loans, dragged the payment, broken the agreed regulations and earned poor ranking in latest cases. You will probably do the same to them. By the way, your payment history sums up to 35% of your total credit score going by FISCO's score analysis, so it would be hard to even make it to average without an impressive payment history.

b. **Credit Mixing Record:** Credit Mixing record is very important too. Your potential creditors often like to confirm whether you have run different credit accounts at different times; whether you can *credit mix* (Run different loans together and pay consistently). The types of credits you have had earlier and how you paid them, in comparison with what you are asking now. Credit mixing wins you 10%.

c. **Credit Record:** Your potential creditors want to know how experienced you are in the game. So, they read up your credit history, find out how long you've been in it and how well. It's a great idea to keep one credit account and maintain it, rather than open various ones. They also want to know whether you have run only *revolving credits* all your life and you suddenly appear for *installment credits* or vice versa. How much you depend on your credit, especially *revolving credit*. They want to be sure whether your business is built on loans, not capital (which earns negative ratings). Whether you pay nothing without your revolving credits and so forth (which is also bad).

They also want to confirm how much debt you are having at the moment (having just a little debt is ideal). This is all documented in the *Trade Line* of your credit report. Do you remember what a trade line is? If you don't, you might have to flip a few pages back to the first chapter. And remember, having good stats here wins you no less than 30% of your credit report too.

d. **Public Judgments:** You remember the third section of your credit report. That's where they can read up all legal judgments you have received on issues related to finance especially. They can tell whether you have just been handed some heavy fine, you have at some point involved in credit scandal et cetera. It's just the spot to discover it all. It is necessary to avoid financial scandals. If you have a lot of that already, now you know what's been scarfing down your credit scores, and will continue to until full seven years when they can be taken off your credit reports.

e. **Other Credit Inquires:** Credit companies are interested in their competitors. They are usually keen to find out the other firms you have contacted for credits and why, probably because they pay faster, charge less or offer some services which this company does not. They also read up the decisions of that firm at that moment. But that's not all, they want to find out how many firms you have tried reaching at each point you needed some funds too. Reaching two each time you need some funds isn't bad, but anything more can attract negative markings.

Just so you know, your credit history, credit mix, and payment history can drastically affect your credit score. Your public judgment of course, so pin them in your heart when you negotiate.

How to Calculate your Credit Score

Many people do not have any idea about how to calculate their credit scores. Some who understand are barely available to teach the others too. This is why this aspect; *how to calculate your credit score* is extensively discussed in the next few paragraphs:

Only five factors have to be considered when measuring your credit score. They were briefly mentioned in the last section and they would be fully regarded below.

a. **Payment History**: This is a statistical analysis that gives information on your previous payment history. How regularly did you pay the agreed dues, how committed and regular were you in each case, how well you met the deadline, etc. Having impressive records here sums to about 35% of the total credit score. How many have you got left to account for? 65%

b. **Your Credit State**: This is similar to finding out your financial state. Have you got debts at the moment? How much does it amount to? How many are they? Do you have the wherewithal to take them on and even add another? How soon will you be done with the current loans? Having little debts, stable financial records and such positive reports in your Trade Line can win you up to 30% of your financial trade. That means after these two factors, all you have left amounts to only 35%.

c. **Credit Account Age**: Here is one other feature usually considered. It is a statistical analysis of how long you have been in the business, how long you have been taking up loans and how experienced you are to handle just another one. This sums up to 15% of your credit score, while the last two factors share 20%.

d. **Recent Reports on your Account**: Is it obvious that you have been visiting a lot of credit companies for help? I remember saying it's not a great idea. Have you been involved in legal or financial scandals; have you been handled your previous interactions competently? They are top stories your creditors want to find out before adding 10% to your accumulated results.

e. **Credit Mix**: Lastly, how are you able to pay up different loans together? What does your record say about that? You know, it is quite difficult to engage in only one credit transaction. For example, there are credit cards, home utility bills, and installment credits like a mortgage, an auto loan and so forth which you have to pay up simultaneously at some point. It is called Credit mixing. Have you hampered one for the other? Credit companies are usually keen on finding that out. Then, they grade your last 10% based on your success level.

As you can see, as much as five factors have to be considered. They bear different percentages of your credit score and you can tell how important each of them is by the number of percentages allocated to it.

You may sketch this yourself now and then. Each point is vital, make what you can.

No Credit Score? The Way Forward

Do you notice anything? We have spent all the time talking about credit statistics. I told you how and why you should change from poor credit scores to impressive ones so you'd raise your chances of getting nice credit deals. But we haven't tried mentioning how to start as someone who doesn't even have a credit account. Well, I have pended talking about that till now. So, if you do not have a credit account at all and you are wondering how to begin, the next few lines are going to be a lot of help to you.

First, you need to have a credit account. No matter how simple or what type, you need to begin with something. Sometimes, you do not need the little amounts but a bigger amount, you can easily build your credit score for bigger funds by withdrawing smaller credits and promptly returning them. It is a practical situation too. You have run your business all by yourself, without anyone's money. There are chances that you will find it hard to adjust to paying schemes, timetables and so forth since you are not used to them from the start. It might be hard to convince lenders if you want a huge loan at some point and they want records which you don't have. You are not so different from those with bad credit scores, since you have zero records yourself.

To avoid such disheartening situations, some methods are in place for citizens of the United States already. The options include:

1. **Finding a Co-signatory**: The easiest way you can get out a nice loan and start building your credit record is to find

an experienced co-signatory. Check around, there should be a couple of reliable friends, family or business associates who have pleasant credit records and will be to stand in as a surety for you. To do this, you need not have any credit record yet, but right, your co-signatory must. An impressive one at that. The loan reflects on the credit records of both of you and can be an amazing start for you if you pay by the contract. You know what it means to you and your partner's record if you fail to meet the standards. This is your best shot if you need the funds urgently.

2. **Getting a Credit-building Loan**: If you are not in an urgent need for credits, it is a good idea to start building your records when you have all the time and resources to get good scores. Start with a credit building loan. What's that? A kind of loan plan which is mainly designed to help you build a great credit record. You can get them from local banks around you and possibly credit unions. And how does it work? You are issued a loan, mainly to help you build your credit record, and a credit bureau is duly notified. The loan is not handed to you. Rather, it is kept in a separate account and you pay it all up according to agreed terms. After payment, the fund is issued to you and the credit bureau considers how you have paid the funds to score your credit report. That means you can conveniently build a credit record with remarkable scores, all at your convenience.

3. **Getting Controlled Revolving Credit Cards**: You may also start a build-up with simple credit cards. Here's how. Just request credit cards from your retail companies. A lot of them offer that. The gas station, the cafeteria, the boutique, etc. You can easily apply and get these cards from them. Then keep your funds, rather than pay at every purchase. Use the credit cards instead. Your charges are roughly the same at the month-end if you paid with cash at every purchase, and now, you have built a credit record with them. As long as they forward your credit record to your credit bureau and you pay for all of your purchases by the month-end, you are building an exciting credit score already.

4. **Watch against Identity Theft**: Now this is important! There are high chances of impersonation if you use any of these simple procedures. Possibly, someone has hacked into your profile and ordered services you will be credited for. A staff of one of your crediting companies decides to pull a fast one on some clients or something similar happens. You will be charged for services you haven't purchased, and it might be pretty hard to prove you didn't ask for those things. This is why you must keep a good record of your purchases on credit. When you notice strange charges, get to the appropriate firms immediately.

5. **Build Credit History**: On a pertinent note, I mentioned how vital it is that you get a credit record, and now I will

warn you. Don't just get a credit record. Keep it. Update it. Be sure you build a long and enviable history. You should see to it that all your records are in one profile with the credit agencies, and update it for as long as possible. Old credit history ups your chances of better credits.

Chapter Summary

The focus of this chapter is to increase your awareness of your credit score, and to note what factors can boost in on one hand, and what factors can militate against it on the other hand.

CHAPTER THREE

WHAT TO KNOW ABOUT CREDIT REPORTING AGENCIES

You need some background information to boost your chances of credits. This is something the higher percentage who get poor credit scores don't keep in mind. Your background information is not on your credit alone. It isn't just your credit scores and your credit history. You need to gather some facts about credit reporting agencies and credit unions too. Are you surprised? Well, thousands of other people reading this page are as surprised as you, but that fact remains a fact.

So, what are the points you need to note? Every single one of them will be mentioned in the next few lines. You sure don't think knowing "there is an agency in charge of your credit records" is enough. Shouldn't you know how they operate? Their policies, regulations, financial play rules, rights, your rights and so forth. If you ask me, you need to know the Fair Crediting Reporting acts also.

Let's begin by learning about prominent credit unions in existence and how they operate:

Prominent Credit Unions in the United States Today

Credit Unions are among the most popular organizations in the United States and other civilized societies today. They are specialized groups in the business world who gather to support the finances of their members or qualified individuals. They've been around since the 18th Century. But that was Europe, they made notable impacts in the US in the earlier 19th century but had less acceptance until 1934 when their existence and registration was formally signed into law. Also, a federal governing organization was established for them. They are not usually coordinated by profit-oriented establishments like banks, they are simply gathered to solve the financial problems of their members. It is what you do when you form a credit or thrift organization with your friends or colleagues, set the policies and invite others to join you.

According to *American Banker* records, the number of members in Credit Unions across the US today towers above 110 million. The National Credit Union Administration (the body which registers all the credit union in the U.S.) also reports in a recent release that there are well over 6,000 registered credit unions in the country all through 2019. They are sometimes run by private individuals, states and the federal government. You will find them here and there in all states of the country. Many of them have less than a million members, but a few have millions of contributors. They likely have ATM services across specific locations, and, as you may guess, they do not usually have branches in all states. Except in cases where they have a mind-blowing number of members across all states in the country, which is quite unusual. Rather, they are found in specific regions.

To start with them, you need to meet certain criteria. These criteria are based on the individual credit union, so each of them might have specifications anyone hoping to be their member must meet. However, the known general steps are:

Research: None of them will ask you to research about them, but you don't want to bump into them and realize that they are just not what you set out to find. So, what do you need to be on the lookout for when selecting possible credit unions you can join?

They are all unique in some ways and that's one thing you need to find out before selecting which to deal with. You need to find out the following:

- Are they founded by Labor Unions, Religious Organizations, A specific Business Enterprise, etc.? Are these sects you can relate to?
- Considering your work, your family and your finances, are you eligible to join?
- What's their saving rate in comparison to others?
- When compared with others, what are their lending rates?
- Is deposit insurance available?
- What is their entry or membership charges?
- What are their terms, policies, and policies?
- ATM fees and distance to you?
- Branch location?
- Credit Card Rewards Program?

Registration: You are required to file in your application after you must have made your choice. They usually require registration funds; the prices are rarely equal anywhere. You may create different types of accounts with them too; savings, lending, checking, etc. They likely request your bank history, social, security Number, tax ID, government-issued ID, and such average requests.

A lot of times, those with richer members, or a higher population of members stand a chance of giving better offers. But as you would have seen, that's just one of the factors to be considered. Gathering enough information on all credit unions that catch your fancy can help you trim your choices to those who can serve you best.

Now, you know the factors to consider when choosing your credit unions, let's give a rundown of some popular credit unions before we take on your Credit Reporting Agencies.

a. **Alliant Credit Union**: the first thing you should know about Alliant Credit Union is that it is not the biggest Credit Union in the States. Its finances are not near the largest too, it is ranked the 8th largest in the States. But this Credit Union is the envy of everyone in just one regard, it provides incredible services for its members at very low rates. It is based in Chicago, Illinois, with branches across Texas, California, Virginia. Even though its membership is not open to everyone, it boasts about 400,000 thousand members up to the month of July 2019.

There are no less than 80,000 ATMs and 11 branches in the States in its name. Every member of the *Foster to Success* organization is deemed eligible to be a member, as well as members of its over 150 qualifying organizations. If you live, worship or work in the qualifying areas, you are likely qualified too. You may like to know that membership is open to all blood relatives of a member as well. You can open almost all types of accounts with the credit union and you can be sure their charges are the cheapest you can get anywhere. With their mobile applications, it becomes easier to navigate and use the services of this organization too.

b. **Navy Federal Credit Union**: By the records, this union is the largest Credit Union in the United States in 2019. Whether you choose to rank them by the population of members or resources, they remain the country's grandest. It was established by the government, not members. But like the Alliant Credit Union, the members of its directory board are selected from the general members. It is a Vienna-headed organization with members everywhere in the country. It has over 8.5 million members, with as much as 17,000 employees and over 250 branches across the country. Also, the ATMs are not less than 500.

It mainly began as a credit union for members of the Navy in Vienna only. But that's not the story today. Apart from including other Navy teams across the country, it includes all members of the Department of Defense in general. It includes the Department's reservists like the Marine Corps, the Navy and the Air force too, whether retired or active. The National Guard personnel including the civilian employees are all included. Employees of the organization and their families are all included. It offers virtually all financial services you may need. Their interest rates are usually less when compared with Banks, and that's a reason they are the first choice for many.

If you are not directly qualified by profession, you should go over your family lists and see if anyone is actively enrolled in the organization and you may get a membership with their influence.

c. **State Employees Credit Union**: With about 2.3 million members, this is one of the largest unions to reckon with in the country. It is based in North Carolina, and as expected, membership is limited to citizens of North Carolina. Despite this limitation, there are at least 260 active branches across the country and the union, according to NCUA, is the second largest in the United States up to the third quarter of 2019.

As long as you are a citizen who works, worships or lives in their location, you are considered eligible for membership. Your immediate families who are not very distant are qualified too. And that's not all. Members of staff and their immediate families can join the credit union. With about 82 years of active services (in 2019), this credit union has been around for a long while, with impressive records of customer services. As long as you are in North Carolina, you will likely find its branches, their ATMs, and virtually all services you need here and there. They are right under your nose, always there to listen to you and that's why a lot of citizens prefer to run at least one account with the union even if they run accounts in other credit unions.

d. **Connexus Credit Union:** Would you like to choose a credit union based on their ATM policies? Then you should be considering Connexus Credit Union. Currently among the largest in her province, the home branch of this union is sited in Canada. And it sees to it that members can use no less than 54,000 ATMs across the country. The ATMs are not only available; they are also fee-free because they are available on a co-op network. If you are the type who enjoys traveling and you need love to use a credit card which has enough ATM stands to withdraw anywhere in the country, then this is just what you are looking for.

Besides their ATM policies, they are also known in the business for unbelievably simple interests on loans. Either for installment or revolving loans, you can bank on them for prices most credit unions cannot beat. You probably have a couple of friends who prefer to draw their mortgage or auto-loan plans with them already. You stand a bigger chance if you run a checking account with the union, and as it stands, membership is vast and international.

e. **First Tech Credit Union:** The list will be incomplete if a credit union like this isn't included. Wondering why? Well, this is one of the few credit unions with staggering records in the world. To start with, it is the first financial institution to render telephone services and online banking, a feature many credit unions and some local banks still struggle to establish today. It is one of the few credit unions whose major objective is technological development and have, by that virtue, supported numerous technological advancements. It is a federal credit union, and it is one of the few credit unions that anybody who desires membership can pick it up.

It was established in Oregon originally, but, according to NUCA'S 2019 statistics, it has 40 branches across Washington, California, Colorado, and Oregon. Also, there are over 5000 partner branches across the country, and 30,000 fee-free ATMs across the country for all members.

Apart from the average credit union services, First Tech offers standard banking services, tax services, investment, mortgage, insurance, and such similar services. There's always a way the union can help, and that's a reason to consider pinning her name on your list.

f. **Golden1 Credit Union:** Golden 1 credit union was established in Sacramento, California in the 1930s. Its membership is limited to the citizens of California, and it boasts about a million members at the moment. It is reputable for charging no monthly fee or the minimum amount which many unions require to create an account in the U.S. Its famous plans for teenagers are why most members and young citizens who often grow used to having it as their credit account, and as such, do not bother to change in many cases.

In a unique style, its recent policies allow teenagers to run a free checking or savings account. They have to co-own the account with a person well considered by the legal system, although they may perform basic transactions without their partner. It performs the basic investment, tax, checking and savings deposit of an average citizen. Among other features of the union, its shared ATM policy makes it possible for members to also withdraw from 30,000 ATMs in the country.

These are among the most sought-after credit unions in the country. To draw your attention to a few others that may also meet your needs; there are Pentagon Federal Credit Union, Langley Federal Credit Union, and GTE Financial Credit Union which is especially for children. In most cases, you require a little amount to register, ranging from $5 to $25, and you are heavily penalized for non-sufficient funds when on loan. So, you should look to avoid that. Due to the ever-changing nature of policies in each organization, you should contact them to find out more when you think you need more information.

Now that you are familiar with your Credit Unions, the most important organizations to learn about is Credit Reporting Agencies.

The Crediting Reporting Agencies

The crediting reporting Agencies, also called the credit bureaus, are special organizations in charge of your credit record. They are specialized firms that have the license to collect and gather your financial information, for future use. They are authorized by various Acts to collate and evaluate your credit records, financial history, and your personal information for near future reference. Such information is then sold to a firm you have contacted for credit, the court, your financial-keeping firm, your insurance company and of course, yourself. It provides a bit-by-bit analysis of how you have accumulated, handled and paid-up loans over a while.

It is important to add, there are only three notable companies in the United States who handle such tasks:

a. **Equifax**: Equifax started as *Retail Credit Company* in 1899, since when it has been compiling records of American and Canadian Citizens. Its services were commercialized in the 1970s and it has gone one to keep records of no less than 800 million people and millions of businesses. There are four basic information it sells; the analytics, demographic data, credit reports, and software. It is interesting to note that the company keeps your financial data, besides your credit report.

The company has performed impressive activities over a long period. However, it is prey to cyber infiltrations and cannot be entirely trusted in recent times. As a practical example, the profiles of over 147 million members were hacked into in 2017, according to the New York Times. The personal data, credit card information, social security numbers etc. were hacked into, and, as a result, the company was heavily fined. There are chances something unobvious may be happening again, so you need to keep track of your financial activities and see to it that they tally with the reports you get from your credit company, Equifax and other financial institutions.

b. **Experian:** Experian is the youngest of the big three. It was established in 1996, only 23 years to 2019. Her activities span across the various fields Equifax works on, and that is the reason the firm can also keep your credit records. It has headquarters in Nottingham in England, Dublin in Ireland, and California in the United States. As you would expect, it is most active in those countries, with no less than 200 million records of US citizens. Experian Plc similarly recorded a massive breach in 2015, among others. In spite of that fact, Experian is recognized in many other countries, and she records the credit of over 1 billion people and businesses on her profile.

c. TransUnion: Transunion is the third largest credit recording company in the United States. Well beyond the shores, it is a working name in 30 different countries at least. It was established about 51 years ago (as of 2019), but it is the smallest of the currently, judging by the statistics. While creating credit reports, it simultaneously offers fraud protection products to users. Ironically, the company, like the other two, has had a tough time wriggling itself out of verdicts on wrong profiles, misrepresentation of individuals, etc. On a general level however, TransUnion is one of the largest, most reliable and efficient credit companies in the United States.

All that said, you should get some other vital details now. Credit Unions, the kinds of credits available and credit information have been mentioned earlier and I firmly believe you can walk up a credit company to look up your credit reports. But what are the rights you can claim before these firms?

The Fair Credit Reporting Act (FCRA) and Its Implication for You

Acts are policies brought up by a state primarily to address a specific issue. It is usually detailed in the constitution of that state. Each Act is expected to address a particular issue in a particular way. You will agree that is true if you pick a copy of any standard constitution and consider the details supplied by the Acts. What is the fair credit reporting act?

It is a detailed regulation brought up and enforced by the federal government to see to it that each credit is collected, compiled and used legally and properly. The Act makes us that your basic rights are considered when collecting or submitting your credit information to anyone. In the United States Constitution, Title section 1681, the Fair Credit Reporting Act is declared and described in detailed. It covers how your Credit Reporting Agencies should go about collecting information, what kind of information they should collect about you, how long they can keep the information, when and who can collect your information, among many other data.

According to the FCRA:

The following personal information may be collected by the credit bureaus;

- Location
- Your Bill Payment History (From your major and minor crediting firms)
- Legal and Criminal records
- Past Loans
- Current Debt
- Employment Details

Only the following people are allowed to access your credit information with your consent:

- Yourself
- Your Insurance Company
- The government
- A potential lender
- Your potential Employer/ landlord etc.

None of these entities reserve a right to request for your credit information, except when there is a specific situation at hand that requires it for verification, and you fully consent to its procurement.

What are the implications of the FCRA on you?

Your (the consumer's) right are fully described and they include the following:

a. You have a right to see your credit report at least once a month. Therefore, you can request a copy from any of the credit reporting agencies. You may also request straight from annalcreditreport.com, the official CRA site.
b. You have a right to confirm the credit report drafted by each agency to confirm its veracity. Remember you have discovered that these firms are not safe from cyber infiltrations and misrepresentation. You should ensure you review and verify any credit report to be forwarded to any firm that requests your information.
c. You have a right to move negative information such as criminal records, bankruptcy etc. off your credit information after seven years.
d. Your credit bureau must inform you the moment they observe something is not right in your credit.
e. You have a right to forward any inconveniences caused by your credit bureau to the Federal and Consumer Financial Protection Bureau.

With these points ringing in your mind, you can now flip to the next page to discover the answer to one of the most controversial issues you have heard: credit Vs debt.

Chapter Summary

There are three major credit reporting agencies that provide you with free annual report of the status of your credit. This chapter reveals their modus operandi and tells you every other factor you should consider as you deal with them and the credit repair companies.

CHAPTER FOUR

THE RELATIONSHIP BETWEEN DEBTS AND CREDIT

A lot of students want to know. Businessmen want to be sure they are not mixing up terms. University Scholars would endlessly argue about it, **Debts VS Credits, are they the same?**

It might be pretty hard to tell whether these terms are different or not, considering how aptly one substitutes the other in the mouth of many language users. That's mil. It gets more complex when you consider how a lot of lexicographers choose to define these words as synonyms of each other. But note a line of distinction, what they defined are *words*, not *terms* and on that ground, they are right. But in the business world where these words are technically used, there is a thin and silver line of distinction between them. What does that imply? They are not the same, but they are words that function in related fields. Do you remember 'borrow' and 'lend' in the orthographical grammar? You will agree, *borrow* isn't the same as *lend*, and *lend* cannot substitute *borrow*, we are talking about the same thing here.

Credit is the total amount available to be given out to a person found worthy, on the condition that he pays according to agreed regulations. You remember that clause you hear when your credit card's customer service agent sits in front of you, your new credit card in her outstretched hands while she says. '*Mr. Grezen, I have to tell you a thousand dollars ($1000) is the maximum amount you can withdraw from your credit card each month*'. Do you remember moments like that? That's what I'm talking about. The total amount possible for you to get on loan is your credit. What's the credit balance on your credit card? The total amount you have on your credit card isn't always the problem. The problem in fact, is your debt.

So, what's your debt?

That moment you have decisively taken out funds, from a crediting company, a friend or relative on a mutual condition you will pay up according to certain terms and conditions, you have taken on debts. As a practical example, you got $45 from a friend, $65 from *Pops*, $250 from a company and paid for a $100 worth pair of shoes with your credit card. You have successfully heaped debts of various origins on yourself. You should paint this picture in your mind now. If you do not withdraw from your Credit Card, your credit remains in there and you will not be charged for it when the month ends. The same goes for every other debt you have taken. They remain credits when they are available but yet to be drawn out, and *debts*, the instant they are drawn.

By the way, if you have drawn out all those debts mentioned in the last paragraph, then it looks like you have a lot to spend when the month ends. So, you understand the relationship between Credit and Debt and you understand Credit VS Debt now? Amazing, I just knew you would!

Now that you can differentiate credit and debt, let's give the details of another part of a debt, the good and bad debt.

The Good and Bad Debt

How does it feel to talk about debts? From a research work I started alongside two Doctoral students of a University in North Carolina, we are yet to finalize facts, but it is becoming apparent that most people naturally hate the idea of debts. *Express Funds*, a TV show decided to sample people's opinions on the same issue, so they requested everyone to give their views on taking loans in one of their shows. Foreseeably, about 60% of respondents consider taking loans a bad idea. '*The credit unions tax your life out of you!*' a woman screamed on the phone. Another one lamented she's taken personal loans and she can't breathe without worry till she pays up the last penny. Men mostly complained about credit cards. They simply can't explain how they end up with such cutthroat debts when the month ends. But did you notice something? As much as 40% disagree, that's pretty high!

When asked, they mentioned how they wouldn't have got their home or car if they hadn't gone on a mortgage and they feel convenient to pay up their loans. If 40% of respondents do not see taking debts as a bad idea, then debt is not always a bad idea, and neither is it a good idea because 60% of respondents cannot be considered clueless.

Here's where it gets interesting, some of the debts are bad and some are good. How? What are good debts and what are bad debts?

Good debts

A lot of times, you suddenly feel the urge to achieve something huge in your family, in your career or as a long-term investment. You will likely start pacing the room, your hand in your head, furiously thinking about where to get such a huge amount you require. Finally, you decide to get a loan from friends, relatives or a specialist.

You may be planning to:

- Invest in your business
- Startup a new business
- Pay up some running costs required to make your products
- Send your kids to college or attend college yourself
- Get some types of machinery for your business
- Merge or buy up a folding business
- Commercial Real Estate Investments
- Mortgage etc.

You can imagine the sort of urgency you would feel in your body system if you have to make payment for any of the above items. You would be ready to loan from anyone because you are sure that getting these things can bring you long term returns. If you eventually get such funds, you would hardly mind the interest because you are sure you have invested the funds in something productive that you can see, sense and hold on to for as long as possible. Even at those moments you feel the burden of paying such high prices, you can always take a long look at what you spent the funds and console yourself; *"come on, it's worth it!"*. Economic Analysts prefer to call these kinds of loans "Installment loans". They are usually made on purchases you cannot eat or use up immediately, instead, they are available for a long while.

Bad Debts

Bad debts are the most common type of debts in the world today. According to *the "American Express" survey* in New York, 2018, 55% of debts are incurred from Revolving Credits. This means that the higher percentage of these loans are incurred from simple transactions. Such Transactions are not long-term in most cases. When they are, they depreciate quickly. Most products or services that cannot be enjoined for a long period purchased with loans like this. We are talking about debuts incurred on the following:

a. **Vehicles**: Getting loans for vehicles, except of course vehicles for business transportation, isn't a great idea. Right, you need some means of transportation. You need a faster route to work, and you want to move at your convenience. But getting a long-term loan remains a bad idea. If you are sure you can pay up these loans in a short while, perhaps, 3-6 months, then it isn't a bad idea. You must bear in mind, however, that vehicles and such facilities require running and maintenance costs. This means you would always have to pay for car services, maintenance, etc. They are costs that can get unreasonably sometimes, and meeting that up doesn't get easier with debts at hand. It would require more maintenance and repairs, perhaps, to be changed before you pay up your credits.

b. **Consumables**: Isn't it hard to believe? Empirical researches show us that consumables are the highest ways people procure loans. People draw up loans, use credit cards, force their loved ones to use their credit cards to purchase consumables and procure extra debts. What are consumables? Products that can be purchased and consumed in a short while. Food, drinks, dress, shoes, groceries, vacation and such similar items. A lot of research points that people do not usually get consumables because they need them in most cases, rather, they feel attracted to the consumables and could not resist the urge to brandish their credit cards, you can always pay this sometime after all.

Evaluate yourself, what are the bad debts you incur unnecessarily? How are you going to put a stop to them?

There you see, Good debts VS Bad Debts. Have you engaged in Good debts? Do you still have the investment around you? Are there debts you have incurred and you are not sure how to group them? You don't think they are good and they are not what anyone calls bad. Anyone like that? Well, debts like that are possible, and they would include the following:

a. **Credit Card Reward Programs**: A lot of times, people decide to stay within their credit limit and not use their credit cards unnecessarily. It's probably happened to you before, right? But your credit card company announces some fantastic rewards out of the blues. You use the card up to this point and you win this or stand a chance of winning it. You ever been in that shoe? Of course, that's not a good loan, neither is it a bad loan. It is a mutual loan that you are sure will cover up for the interests accrued with the incentives attached by your credit company. That could include a gift, a ticket, and so on. The costs of such a reward cover your interests and you haven't incurred a good or bad debt.

How to Manage your Credits

Trying to keep your credits under control can be both tasking and frustrating. You don't ever seem to know what exactly you bought and how you accumulated such an outrageous charge. You have probably drafted some theories and tried to work them out. Painfully, you could not continue the week after. You tried so hard to work it out and but you just cannot explain how it went haywire. You tried to employ another strategy but nothing seems to work correctly. Don't be surprised, you are simply one of the hundreds of millions who cannot hold their peace when the monthly notification arrives. They would pace their room and rack their brains, trying to find an answer to a question that does not exist. The truth is that you haven't applied the actual solutions, perhaps because you don't notice them.

Not to worry, the solutions have been listed in the next few lines, be sure you painstakingly follow them:

a. **Make a firm decision**: Making a firm decision is the top task you have got to make. Decide to be prudent and stand by your decision. You shouldn't jump at the opportunity to use a credit card every time. Be sure what you decided to get is worth being purchased in the first place.

b. **Select a Comfortable Credit Card**: As I have made known to you earlier, there are at least 6000 credit unions for you to select from in the country. You cannot possibly meet the requirement of every one of them. But there are high chances you will at least fancy 1,000. Out of that, you've got about 40 that suit you best. Picking the best of them should be your priority when selecting a credit company. The ideal credit card companies do not make monthly charges. They virtually offer all the services you need. They offer very low interest on loans and their ATMs are often free. Your best credit company shouldn't be far from your home too.

c. **Live within your means**: It is okay to have the crazy urge to bag home the sparkling shoes you found up the mall, or perhaps the red dress you saw in the store. After all, you can always sort the debt with your credit company when the time comes. But if you do this all day, you should be prepared to pay more than you earn. That's because you will likely spend more than you earn each month and that sequels months of endless debt payment in inconveniences.

d. **Draft a Budget**: Drafting a budget is something you probably don't take seriously. Like many other people, you assume a budget is not so necessary and the few times you draft one, you make a lot of purchases like it doesn't even exist. That is one habit you must stop in some way if you want to manage your credit. You need to have a documented data on what would be bought and what wouldn't be in each month. That's not all, you need to stick to it at all times. Whatever you figure you'd like to get that doesn't appear in your budget would be added in subsequent ones. You will be surprised how much you can save from your budget.

e. **Avoid loans when you can:** I strongly advise that you take loans only when there are pressing needs. In most cases, our needs are not pressing and we can always find a way around them. When we find ways around them, we realize the loan need not be drafted in the first place, and it is eventually avoided. In the end, less debt is incurred and credit is reasonably managed.

f. **Keep the records straight:** You shouldn't make the mistake of leaving it all to your crediting companies, your bank, and your credit report agencies. There is always the need for your contribution. Get involved, find out more, check with them all. Do they keep the facts and figures intact? Maintenance is a very vital feature of management. You do not want to make up to strange figures on your credit report and begin to wonder if you ever did make those purchases or they were framed. But you have no right to disprove them because you have no record yourself and you cannot trust your doubt. The last point to disclose to you here is; as you confirm your records with them, create a personal record and keep updating it as you use your credit card.

With a well-managed credit card and proper insight into what credit, credit bureau, credit union, and Fair Credit Reporting Act entails. You stand a better chance in the global market, believe me.

Chapter Summary

This chapter discusses the relationship between debts and credit, the differences between good and bad debts, and the relationship between your credit score and your debts. It also reveals how to manage your credit in the face of debts.

CHAPTER FIVE

FIFTEEN CREDIT SCORE MYTHS TO UNLEARN

People are not always right. But they talk about everything, include credit scores. You have probably heard some damning information you do not know how real they could be. Your sixth sense keeps saying they are too good to be true. In other cases, you have probably heard it all, taken it all and believe they are true, but that doesn't change it from being fallacies either.

Is there any way this book can help then? Definitely! Depending on whom you ask, there are various myths concerning Credit Scores, and here in this book, we will talk about the top 15 myths people pass around on Credit Scores. No matter what part of the country you stay, you have likely heard most, if not all of these myths and it is about time you changed how you view them.

1. **'I have a good credit score since I don't have a credit card debt**: That is wrong! Your credit card is supposed to reveal your credit history, and you have credit history only when you have or have had debts. This is why it is not bad in anyway to have debts in your credit report. Contrary to that perspective, it is possible to have debts in your credit report and still have excellent credit scores. Wondering why? It is because a credit score is not particular about whether you have loans at that moment or you don't. You may have completed your loan payments, but you paid at rather odd, late and uncomfortable times that have violated the agreed

regulations of the contract. In a case like that, you have paid up your debts, but you cannot have a great credit score.

Rather than that, a credit score would evaluate the debts you have taken up, how you honored the deal, how soon and how consistent you paid them up. That means that if you have debts you are paying during the period your credit score is being computed, your debt will be evaluated according to the contract. It will look to find out when you started the contract, the agreed payment schedule and how much you have played by the rules in the pact.

2. **'My credit score reduces every time someone calls for my credit report'**: This observation requires a careful approach. For one reason, your credit score indeed stands to be affected as a result of how often the credit report is requested. But it doesn't affect your credit scores the way you assume it does. First, you should remember the four phases of a credit score. The personal section, the trade lines, judicial reports and lastly, the section for the different individuals or firms who have recently requested your credit report. You will also remember that the last section of your credit record, where those who requested for credit report recently are highlighted carries about 10%.

This means the number of people who have reviewed and within what period will have effects on your score. For example, you will likely get strong marks here if only two have recently reviewed your credit report in 3-6 months. In order cases, your scores reduce if more people have requested for it. This is to tell you that your credit score does not reduce every time someone calls for your credit card, but it will reduce when too many people have called for your card.

3. **'You should deliberately refuse to balance your credit card month by month-end'**: What many people heard was that it is really bad of them to pay up all debts accumulated with their credit card by the month-end. Rather, they should extend the debts to the other months at one time or another. This way, at least, they can keep in touch with debts and build experience of lengthier and complicated debts, and not to worry, it won't affect their credit record in anyway.

   That seems quite awkward and hard to believe. Whether they are simple or complex loans is not even what matters, additional charges will be placed on your credit the moment you withdraw more than your credit limit in the month. That is not all, you will incur the last thing you want to have; poor credit scores. As far as the records prove, there is no known benefit of trying something like that, instead, everybody believes it has got negative impacts only. So, you need not try out theories and tales that could place you in financial difficulty. If you must experiment with something new, make sure it isn't this.

4. **'Your credit score cannot be easily spoilt'**: You will probably hear some boasting about how they are so sure your credit score can't get affected so easily. A lot of them think your credit reporting agencies would usually overlook the simple errors you make, the few debts you delayed, and the credit card charges you pended as long as you do not continue for a very long time. I find this very interesting. Having known for sure that these things are myths people try to picture in their heads so they could hold on to some hope when they make mistakes. They would usually boast about how they are sure little debts, little errors and little recklessness can't do much harm. They often extend the duration of their loans. They don't feel the urgency to pay up their credit card charges as soon as they can too.

You honestly do not want to join that crew. Their ideas are simply unrealistic and preposterous. Credit Bureaus are charged to record every fact and figure, and they must put them all into consideration when grading your credit performance in the year. If you had had impressive records in these little records, would you want them overlooked?

5. **'If you have poor records, there's no way you can have a turnaround again'**: It is surprising to see that quite a lot of people believe this. They fear that there's no way anyone who has poor credits can have a turnaround. According to many, the poor records continue to linger in the records, and as such cannot be erased. Some others believe that it is always difficult to overwrite any bad record on a credit score. It drags down your grade and makes it extremely hard to make high scores, always battling with the positive activities that could add to their grades.

But on an entirely different perspective, it is interesting to note that such policies are too bad to be true. They are unfound fallacies, and stories that are not near accurate. Poor records are not permanent on your profile. The only reason they become permanent is if you repeat the same activities that got you bad grades from the start. For example, you got an auto loan from A&D Inc., agreed to pay up in six months but extended the payment till about 10 months. You are bound to earn a low credit score with that, but if you perform better in other loans, your credit report will be gradually boosted.

6. **'You can't ever remove your bad records'**: This is one of the reasons many people feel they need to start again. It occurs a few times that you have a long and impressive credit history, but finances became harsh and some point and you couldn't go on with the payment policies on loans you have drawn earlier. You will likely earn poor grades with that, but when evaluated alongside your old records, you realize you still stand a chance. In some cases, these poor records go on for a long while that they fill your profile and you doubt whether you can ever wriggle out of them.

For some, they have more than enough poor records of payment on their profile and at some point, they began to keep up with things. They earned more and they paid their loans better, but their new records are always downed by their old records. In either case, you will likely feel tempted to open a new credit account. Particularly if you believe the poor records will always lurk in your profile. Many people jettison their venerated profiles and take on new ones, therefore finding it very challenging to secure the trust of new credit companies.

In most cases, you do not have to do that. Whether you make further credits or not, whether you have impressive records afterward or not, the United States Fair Act mandates that after seven years, you can remove a poor record from your profile permanently, which means it will no longer be considered or referenced in your credit card or credit score.

7. **'There is just a credit score for you'**: This assumption is usually made by people who are just arriving into the credit arena, and perhaps of course, some older ones paying little attention. They assume that only one credit score is for them in many instances, and therefore do not see the need to pursue others. They believe what you get from TransUnion will likely be the result from Experian and so forth. They also believe that the same grading method is used. In truth, there are different models and different credit reporting agencies. If they work exactly then there really may not be the need to have more than one. As a practical example, it is possible to be graded 780 of 1000 if graded by Experian, and you get 830 when graded by TransUnion. You can then decide who forwards to your crediting company or what you send to them if they are accustomed to a particular company.

So, starting with your Credit Bureaus, be sure that you will always get different results from different organizations. Besides that, there are various models used in grading your credit scores too. FICO is the most used, and definitely what you are familiar with, but there are a couple of others like Credit Xpert, CE credit score, TransRisk, Vantage, and so many others. While they are fairly similar, each of them works in a unique style and you would get different scores from each of them, which may in spite of that, be in a range.

8. **'Employers consider credit scores in employment'**; Because many companies request the credit report of their applicants, many believe they use the credit scores generated in the credit report to evaluate their potential employers and sometimes grade how responsible they would be at work. *Financial crossroads* reports that many even assume the sole reason employers request credit report is to review how much their applicant has been in debt, and could at any time abscond with the company's finances.

These are all absurd claims that have been on the street for such a long time. But tales like this must not get into your head. You simply can't afford to believe them. You can relate to this by considering yourself the Employer, would you turn down an impressive application simply because the applicant is in debts? Don't we get work to clear our bills and live comfortably? It is how everyone lives.

Most employers only request credit reports because they would like to confirm the basic data about you. Are you an existing, active member of the community? They have an idea how much you need the job too, while confirming your facts on your finances, and that's all there is to it.

9. **'Having a lot of money in the bank boosts your credit** score': Another myth going on in the minds of people about credit scores is about bank accounts. Many feel that once they have some huge cash in their account, it can be rated alongside their credit scores and in some way, they should get much better grading. Without even being asked, many would attach their bank details or tax information to their credit reports when presenting it themselves. To some, having enough in your bank means you really have been finding your way off incurring debts. So, you have avoided using credits and you should be awarded pretty high credit high scores. But that's not near the case your credit score is your credit score. It is not your financial score. It is meant to supply information on your credit, not your finances as a whole, so having a large bank account says nothing about getting very high scores. Do you want high scores? Play by the rules, there's no two-way.

10. **'Paying off an old debt saves your credit score'**: Humans are especially intelligent beings. Some way, they are sure that they can always bend a few rules and get exactly what they want. It is the reason they would believe that a few days to when their credit report would be submitted, they could pay up old and overdue debts on

their file and get the high scores they deserve from the start. Many often forget that the scores are not calculated by finding out whether the debt is fully cleared or not, rather, by measuring how much the policies are obeyed.

Here's what I am reiterating. You got an auto loan in January 2109, with a six-month regulation which means you should pay up the funds by July 2019. Due to errors solely on your part, you could not pay up the funds at that moment. You still have some amount of the loan left to be paid when in November 2019, you desire to take up a mortgage loan with another firm. Contrary to popular belief, paying such loans at that moment do not rid you of a bad credit score, as your credit score is projected to display how you played by the agreed regulations within the deadline, not exactly whether you paid up or not. So, if you are assuming paying at such moments can save you in some way, take your mind off it all.

11. **'Bad credit score means the end of your career':** This is another myth I have to talk about at this point. I figure you must have gathered from what you have read so far that having bad credit scores is surely damaging. Success is crucial to having your loans funded. That is exactly how virtually everyone views it, but that's not the case. It is not always the case that you will make no headway with bad scores. Sometimes, they are situations

that can be understood by any potential crediting firm. Once in a while, your credit scores tend to be dissatisfactory, but that is not the end of your career.

A bad credit score doesn't down anyone's chances of a loan to zero. Besides, if you can back your current loan request with a convincing proposal, you stand a fairly better chance. There is therefore no reason to lose hope if you have just hit the worst credit scores in your career. Simply try to maintain clear-cut goals and approach firms who are likely to be more considerate, perhaps because they are in your business line and they understand the complexity of your business. You have similar socio-economic goals or you belong to the same religion. But you must remember that poor credit score isn't near the end of your career, it has only made it slightly stricter to get funds.

12. **'Your poor credit score can't get better until seven years'**: Okay, this is very interesting. I told you that you have the right to erase a bad record from your credit report after it's being there seven years, right? Well, that's true, and that's why some people believe that until that seven years when they can withdraw their poor record from a credit report and of course the credit score, they can't get a better credit score.

By the length and breadth of the research report of all observations, that thinking is not right. Try to think of it this way; if you take new loans, pay them off regularly and do that consistently for such a period that your bad record only weighs little on your total score, why won't you have a great credit score?

It is a very practical situation. You need not wait that long to nurse up a great credit score again. Just take up more loans, within what you can handle of course and do better with them. At that point where you have impressive performances up and down your credit report, you would have such a great credit score that you won't have to wait seven years since your old responses are irrelevant.

13. **'You should check the score only when you apply for a loan'**: This is another myth a lot of people hold onto for no reason. A young secretary was asked in a TV show about her credit score recently. Her response was *'I am not taking any loan right now, so I can't be sure about the state of the credit score'*. *'Who cares?'* was a man's response. Another retorted *'I don't need a loan; why should I carry that in my head?'*

From many more kinds of that research, it becomes pretty clear that a lot of people see no reason they should know what their score is if they are not applying for a loan. They do not request the records or check them until a pressing need appears for some funds. You will find it difficult to cover up your deficits when you do not know how bad until the nick of the period you need it.

You can't ever keep an eye on your progress, pick out the errors and feel spurred to get investors and broaden your business scope if your credit score doesn't ring in your head. It isn't a piece of shit, it is your chance at life, get to it and find out more.

14. **'You can great a poor credit score if you disprove of a credit report':** When Equifax was hacked in 2017, a lot of people were sent their credit scores and their credit reports. About 37% of those whose credit scores were affected were confused. They got fewer scores than they should, but they were worried, assuming what they got was probably right, and what they would get was worse if they complained.

    This isn't just something they developed on the spur of that moment; it was a myth that has been around for ages. People believed that whenever you disprove of a credit report on whatever grounds, you would likely return with much fewer ones. It turns out that this isn't the case, however. People who got fewer credit scores after disproving their credit report probably had more debt than they recorded on their credit report. So, be sure you are not getting fewer credit scores for disproving a credit report, you have every right to sue any credit bureau which you suspect plays games with your reports!

15. **Salary size, support to organizations, etc. affect my credit score**: the assumption that salary size, support to organizations and such large finances outside credit report can affect credit scores is still very much around today. A lot of people often ask in credit and financial seminars I attend, *"If I receive well over a thousand dollars in a month, and I deposit only 150$ as my monthly credit charge. Will I be affected negatively if I do not pay that money in some months and I still receive my salary?* Another would ask, *"Is it in any way possible for my credit report to reflect that I have supported NGOs or make financial donations?*

Many do not bother to ask but simply assume such statistics must be included and would devaluate their credit bureau once they don't find such when their credit report arrives. You need to remember every time that this is a credit report, and no more than a credit report. It will not in any way be influenced by external circumstances. This means having enough money in your account cannot boost your credit score when it is precariously low, and having nothing in your wallet can't reduce your score if you have got an excellent score. Salary size, support to organizations, donations, humanitarian activities, and all sorts can make no entry on a credit score. You want a striking credit score; you know how to get it. Drop the myths!

Now, you have identified some popular beliefs about credit score and how untrue they all are. You have also learned what your credit scores and external factors such as your salary size, bank account, employers, et cetera have to do with one another. Most importantly, we mentioned your credit score, credit errors and how disproving credit errors used to be a tough task to people. What and what are credit errors? Why don't we talk about that now?

Chapter Summary

You have definitely heard a lot about credit report and credit score, both from experts and non-experts alike. Unfortunately, not all of them are exactly right. This chapter is dedicated to disabusing your mind about credit and your credit score.

CHAPTER SIX

CREDIT ERRORS AND DISPUTES

The Federal Trade Commission reports that out of every five credit reports issued in the United States, at least one of them is not right. This situation is described as credit error. A situation where the proper facts and figures expected in your credit report are distorted. You don't find them the way they should be, they are inflated, understated or simply inaccurate. When any of these happens, you have the right to call the attention of the issuing Crediting Bureau and see to it that every error is corrected. To do something like that at all, you need to understand the errors. What can be called an error on a credit report? What can be overlooked? How should you seek amends amicably? Are there ways you can avoid making the same mistake a lot of people made, and as a result do not get a review? You need to see the next few paragraphs for a deep understanding.

Credit Errors

You already have a good idea of what credit errors are. We may simply go on to find out, what the credit errors are that could be found in a credit report.

   a. **Identity Error:** This is a basic report you want to start with. Any error in this invalidates every bit of information in the report, no matter how accurate it seems. What's an identity error like? It is what happens when you open your credit report and you find a misspelled name, a wrongly arranged name, or a different name. That's not all. Your phone number, address and account information are all unique parts of your identity.

By implication, an identity error connotes that whatever is presented in the report belongs to someone else, and that such information has been mixed, hacked or erroneously computed. Such errors can have drastic effects on the account user's accessibility, so, your identity must be verified before anything else.

b. **Wrong Account Update**: Another cogent information you should be quick to check after your identity is your account update. The statement of account must present the same facts and figures you recorded on your own. A reason I often recommend that you keep your credit record while your credit reporting agencies reserve the official copies. You want to be sure that accounts you have closed are not reported as open, your account belongs to you, and not another person with a similar name. You also want to make sure that the account reports your factual position of authority on the account. For example, if you are just an authorized user, you should not be reported as the user. You should also ensure that the same debt is not repeated on your credit list, and the dates of withdrawal, payment are aptly recorded. You also need to confirm whether your account is reported as delinquent or late. By the time you have evaluated such statistics and you do not find them wanting, you are sure the account is yours, and you may find the next type of errors.

c. **Data Management Errors**: Are the data and statistics properly inserted? Are there any repetitions, omissions, additions, or deletions in the data supplied? Not taking note of these factors may also result in a fatal fall in your credit score particularly if a certain debt is listed more than once under different headings. You understand that it is most probably the same debt, but such would be analyzed as another debt that you took at about the same period. Here again, you want to thoroughly go over all that you have read, and confirm whether they are accurate. How about the information you requested for correction earlier, do they still reflect? Seeing that this is all right is important to your fiscal career, you know.

d. **Look Forward to your Credit Report**: If you have identified where the error started, and you have linked all necessary data, you can look forward to a new credit report after the credit bureau must have researched and confirmed your requests. If the error was from the sourcing company, then all bureaus must have made that error and then the firm that produced that information must notify the three major credit bureaus in writing.

e. **Further Official Actions**: After your credit report is corrected and you receive another free copy, your credit

75

bureau is expected to notify anyone who has recently requested and received your credit record, officially within the past six months. In cases that the error has been made on your credit record for a longer period, say two to three years, anyone who has received your credit report within the last six months should be sent a new copy too.

There they are: the steps to reporting an error in a credit report. Remember to strictly follow the instructions. It is the only way you can get some response at the end. I should be quick to add that you may reach these credit bureaus by phone, or online, but you would still be required to send an official letter and enclosures.

How to Write a Dispute letter

Already, you are entirely aware that this has a definite format to follow. Check out the format as outlined by FCRA in the next few lines. But first, you must remember that you need to clearly highlight the items you dispute in your credit report. Add the reasons you do not agree with them as well. You already know you need to back your claims with every file that you can support it with. Lastly, have it clearly stated that you want this error corrected. You also remember we stated that you should send your letter by a certified mail; *return receipt requested*. So, here's the format:

[Your Name]

[Your Address]

[Your City, State, Zip Code]

[Date]

Complaint Department

[Company Name]

[Street Address]

[City, State, Zip Code]

Dear Sir or Madam:

I am writing to dispute the following information in my file. I have circled the items I dispute on the attached copy of the report I received.

This item [identify item(s) disputed by name of source, such as creditors or tax court, and identify type of item, such as credit account, judgment, etc.] is [inaccurate or incomplete] because [describe what is inaccurate or incomplete and why]. I am requesting that the item be removed [or request another specific change] to correct the information.

Enclosed are copies of [use this sentence if applicable and describe any enclosed documentation, such as payment records and court documents] supporting my position. Please reinvestigate this [these] matter[s] and [delete or correct] the disputed item[s] as soon as possible.

Sincerely,

Your name

Enclosures: [List what you are enclosing.]

Do you find it up-front? Right, it is. But if you are not sure you can try this without errors, let's try two sample letters right away. Let's assume, for the first one, that I am Meg GRAY and I have just received my credit report from Equifax. I got to know that the total amount left to pay my crediting company isn't right accurate in the report. I found $5,000 on my credit report and I do not have more than $800 left to pay, having paid $4,200 all at once. Here is what we have:

Meg Gray,

2273 De La Boulevard Santa Clara CA

408

11/12/2019

Complaint Department

Equifax

P. O. Box 740241, Chester, PA Business Bureau Rating

678

Dear Sir or Madam:

I am writing to dispute the following information in my file. I have circled the items I dispute on the attached copy of the report I received.

The total amount left to pay "Keypoint Credit Union", my credit company is inaccurate because I have $800 left to be paid on my credit, and not $5,000. I am requesting that this error be changed to the appropriate information.

Enclosed are copies of my receipts from the previous payments, my total charge and how they have been paid. I have also attached a copy of the most recent notification from Keypoint Credit Union, clearly stating my position that I have only $800 to balance. Please reinvestigate this matter and correct the disputed item as soon as possible.

Sincerely,

Meg Grey

Enclosures: [a receipt from Keypoint issued on the 15th of December, My credit transaction from Keypoint]

In the other case, may name is John Wickham and my report just got here from Equifax too. For reasons I can't fathom, the two reports from other agencies didn't add a thing to my name, but here, I find John Wickham M. '*M.*' isn't part of my name, so that simply cannot be me. I decided to write Equifax, but I note that this error originated from a record of a debt I took up at Keypoint Credit Union. The name on the profile of the other loans is perfect. What do you think I would do? Right? Contact the Information providing company first. I reached Keystone Union and I was made to understand that that error did not erupt from their records. It has to be from the Credit Bureau.

What do you think I should do? Mail the credit bureau of course. And I will do it by a certified mail; *return receipt requested*. Let's sketch it out;

John Wickham

2273 De La Boulevard Santa Clara CA

408

11/12/2019

Complaint Department

Equifax

P. O. Box 740241, Chester, PA Business Bureau Rating

678

Dear Sir or Madam:

I am writing to dispute the following information in my file. I have circled the items I dispute on the attached copy of the report I received.

My profile name as reported in the credit information from Keystone Credit Unions is inaccurate because M. is inaccurately added to John Wickham, as in John Wickham M. I am requesting that this M. be removed and John Wickham, my proper information be maintained.

Enclosed are copies of my opening account slip, final transaction report and monthly payment notification. Please reinvestigate this matter and correct the disputed item as soon as possible.

Sincerely,

John Wickham

Do you still think it is hard? I bet you'd get it.

Chapter Summary

Errors are almost inevitable in credit reports. Find the factors responsible for credit errors in this chapter, and learn how to effectively dispute them. This chapter also provides u=you with typical dispute letter samples for your reference.

CHAPTER SEVEN
WHAT IS CREDIT COUNSELLING?

Credit Counselling is an intervention strategy introduced into crediting when things seemed to be going the last way everyone wanted them to go. It was birthed that a miracle needed to happen in the credit industry. Too many people had run into all forms of debt and they were sure that no matter how much they tried. The debts had gone beyond what they could afford to pay back. Many had turned criminals, breaking other homes to pay their loans, engaging in verbal and intellectual arguments with the credit unions they owed, and dragging one another to courts and taking rounds to seek judgments. In the end, many lost their resources, more became prisoners and a lot of loans cannot be accounted for.

These circumstances were especially popular in the US throughout the 1950s, and it remained that way till creditor banks and credit card companies decided to come together to help these people. The same way they had formed Credit Reporting Agencies (CRA) to compile creditors' data, they decided to form organizations that can help people in financial disarrays out of their loan burdens up to the point that their debts are partially or fully cleared. This led to the establishment of the *National Foundation for Crediting Counselling* in 1951 in the US. The organization became active and handled many more issues in the 1960s. They particularly tended to the growing volume of bankruptcy at that time, and they made incredible contributions.

Shortly after, Credit Counselling came into view in different parts of the world, particularly Europe, where it was more popular in countries like the United Kingdom and Sweden. From the report of several kinds of research, there are alterations in the style and specific functions of credit counselors but some are general. That includes the fact that your credit counselor is an individual whose main responsibility is to consider the precarious situation of your finances and offer you education and suggestions on debt management, assist in drawing up your budgets and negotiating with your creditors to see how debts that you cannot pay will be resolved.

Some of these organizations are Non-Profit organizations and many more are profit-oriented. Often, they charge high prices for their services. A lot of times, they have assisted their clients through their different auto loans, mortgage, credit card loans and debts that they would not otherwise have paid up. Some loans are forgone by the credit firm in a debt relief negotiation initiated by credit counselors. In other cases, they negotiate with a crediting firm to see how the interest on the loans of the clients would be brought to the barest, and see to it that they are billed the little amount they could afford monthly. These situations are regarded as Debt Management Plan in the United States and are known as Individual Voluntary Arrangement in the UK. After the credit companies have agreed and reduced the rates, the total debts of the individual are then merged as a single debt which the clients understand that they must pay.

If you find yourself in a tough financial situation, one of those times the calculations are all running into each other in your head, and you begin to realize you might be staring at some financial crisis in the eye. You are getting worried that you probably would find the coming month's credits hard to pay. It happens a lot of times, and getting you out is the job of Credit Counsellors. They review your financial situation and proffer your best options to you. In the words of McClay, a prominent staff of NFCC, "When you meet a certified counselor, you get expert advice on how you can overcome your biggest financial challenges." It is interesting to note that most credit counseling sessions are held over the phone or on the computer; only a much smaller percentage involves offline interaction.

Do you Really Need One?
A certified credit counselor is trained to give you expert opinions on your credit in particular. This means if you hold no credit record at all, you do not even need a credit counselor. But that is very fair, as you should have credit accounts, as we earlier agreed. If you have got credit accounts on the other hand, probably loans, close-ended loans or credit cards and so on, you can use a credit counselor but it is not in any way mandatory.

Let's talk about this. A lot of people find it relatively easy to think on their own and figure out solutions to their problems. They are their own bosses and they have lived their entire life learning to decide. If that sounds like you, then you cannot go far with a credit counselor. You are likely to take up your own decisions whether it aligns with what the counselor has just suggested or not, and you would act on your decisions only. It may seem a bad idea, but it is just the way of people like that.

For some, however, their financial situation has gone out of hand. They cannot handle their financial imbroglio anymore. They need someone to hear them, and speak with them about money and how to manage it. The best shot of people like that is to get the suggestions and opinions of an expert. *Financial critics*' 2019 magazine also observes that "if people use expert opinions from the moment they obtain their loans or the minute they get their credit cards, they would be half better off than they often were." Why? Because they would not make half the mistakes they often make without a counselor. They would also have well-outlined budgets that could guide their financial life.

But that's not to rule out a fact that a lot of people have deftly operated their credits and debts. They have got themselves out of damning financial situations and remain unbeaten as ever. You surely remember Donald Trump is a living example of that case. As it seems, the only inference you should make is that the choice is all on you. Whether you see a financial or credit counselor is purely on how you feel about it. After all, the services of a financial counselor can be used at any time and you can manage your finances pretty well without them.

What are the services rendered by a credit counselor?

a. **Compiling your Financial Information**: These are not credit reporting agencies you remember, but they compute your financial information too. In fact, they do compute and analyze every data related to your finances (income, expenses, budgets, loans, partnership, and total assets) with you. Unlike credit bureaus, a credit counselor would sit, review and provide expert opinions on your finances. For example, you have different resources worth a million USD, but you owe $500,000. We may choose to assume that you didn't even know you have enough resources to pay up that debt, but now you see. That's not all, you intensely discuss the possible ways you can pay up this debt without eating up a great bulk of your resources. So, first, compilation and analysis of your financial information are what creditors do.

b. **Loan Advice**: The major reason things go out of hands was that you don't make the right decisions at the necessary point. Perhaps, you become pretty sure everything would work out that way, against all odds or you have no idea you are making a grave mistake. Nobody enjoys being in an unfortunate financial situation. Definitely, not me. I guess you don't too. You have probably made one mistake and that's why you seek a counselor. Trained and certified counsellors often do it right. They bail you out with some timed and tactical pieces of advice on your loans. How soon you should think about loans if you have some at the moment, your next chances of loans, and many other related talks.
c. **Making Budget**: While they offer expert opinions on loan drafting, you probably may not enjoy any other service of credit counselors as much as budgeting. Have you seen what a professional budget looks like? This is one of your most certain sources to pick one of them. While they help you to compute a professional budget that you would surely find appealing to follow, they would help you stream down the items on your budget list to the best you can ever have. Usually, you draft a budget containing everything you hope to purchase and present it to them. While you sit and actively participate, they help you streamline your expenditures to the basics. They also strongly advise you to stick by your budget.
d. **Bankruptcy Advice**: Bankruptcy is a financial condition that we will spare all the time to talk about in some of the coming pages. But then, it might interest you to know that it is a heartbreaking condition of finance you surely don't want to

achieve. Bankrupt individuals often have difficulty moving with life. They practically cannot afford anything and they are usually in huge debts. It isn't abominable, however. It is a state that could happen to anyone. Credit Counsellors are specially trained to walk people out of this phase too. Not by funding them financially, but through informed decisions that can help them find their position in the financial world again.

e. **Designing a Debt Management Plan:** Have you heard about Debt Managing Plan? A debt managing plan is a scheme usually proposed by credit counselors to creditors on behalf of their clients. Your credit counseling firm may suggest this to you if you have difficulty keeping up with loan records, paying up or you cannot afford to pay your charges each month. Your credit counseling firm would likely negotiate with each and all of your creditors to cut down their interests and reduce their monthly charges so you can afford to pay them regularly. After talking to all of your creditors and reaching an agreement on when and how much each would be paid, your counseling firm returns to you. An account is opened by the crediting firm, and you are required to pay the total amount due to the account each month, with regards to the new terms and conditions of the loan. It is what many call loan debt consolidations, and counseling firms usually charge a little for it.

f. **Using your Credits to your Benefit:** What is the condition of your finance? How much have you got? What is your withdrawal limit? These and many others are questions that your credit counselor would be willing to discuss with you. They are interested in your chances of using your credit to the extent possible. They also want to see to it that your credit bundles are convenient.

g. **Getting a Debt Settlement Deal for you:** Have you got to a point you honestly need a debt settlement? A lot of credit unions would not even listen to a debtor directly. Besides, bringing in an expert shows you actually desire it, and you had to have someone plead with the banks on your behalf. Getting a debt settlement becomes an option when you have tried all that you can to see the loan paid but none of the efforts paid off. You have got to a brink where if you have to lose your property for not paying a loan. That's the moment getting a debt settlement becomes an alternative. Credit Counsellors can take you through this process.

Chapter Summary

Discover the truths ab out credit counselling and credit counselors. Do you really need a credit counselor? What are the roles and significance of credit counselors? Find out for yourself in this chapter.

CHAPTER EIGHT
THE TRUTH ABOUT BANKRUPTCY: HOW BAD CAN IT GET?

Bankruptcy is a very critical situation that you must understand in crediting. Everyone wants their business to bloom, but once in a while, business owners may need to declare this to save themselves from frustration, mental derailment, prevention of jail terms, criminal conduct, among other things. What is it? Bankruptcy is an official situation where a person declares that they are too poor to pay up their loans and must therefore be helped in some way that would include writing off some of the debts and reducing the interest rates of virtually others.

Bankruptcy is usually fatal on your credit card, and you must have got to that point where it is obvious that there's just no way you will get that money to clear the dues creditors are slamming on your table. You have sold off virtually all that you could; you have borrowed to a level it doesn't make any sense anymore and you are just not getting the money. At that point, it is too hard to get enough to feed yourself and creditors are expectant. You have got no financial hopes too. No investor is forthcoming and there is practically no debtor. Moments like these are not so common, right? But it may happen and you should know what to do if it ever comes. If this happens to a friend too, you know exactly what steps they need to take.

Once you notice you are about going bankrupt, the basic step is to reach out to a credit counselor. Fix an appointment and tell them where you stand. You would likely be exposed to a variety of alternatives to bankruptcy. That includes *the Debt Management Plan*, which I have told you about recently, Debt consolidation and a couple of others. You may, however, resort to announcing Bankruptcy if you think you prefer it, or if it becomes clear that it is all that you have left. In many cases, many debts are cleared using one of those two methods, particularly if they are unsecured loans.

Wondering what unsecured loans are? Well, there are certain terms you need to understand in bankruptcy.

They are:

1. **Secured Debt**: A secured debt is the kind of debt that is issued with a collateral. For example, an auto loan that you were granted and made to understand that at any point you could not pay the funds anymore, the vehicle would be seized as collateral. Vehicle loans, investment and so forth, fall into this category.

2. **Unsecured Debt**: Just the opposite of secured debts, this is the sort of debts you take with no collaterals. Credit cards, a loan from friends, indirect loans, etc. are typical examples of unsecured debts.

3. **Reaffirmed Account**: This is a sort of debt that you retain during bankruptcy. As a case study, O'Neill declared bankruptcy recently and he forfeited his house in the process. But he loves the house and he simply cannot let it go. Therefore, he reaffirms the house and it is not taken off, rather it is deemed one of his resources that cannot be forfeited during his bankruptcy. But the total he is expected to pay increases.

4. **Exempt Property**: No matter how much you have to pay, the state makes sure that some vital property that can help you start living again are not lost in the process. They are called exempt or non-forfeiture property. Usually, each state has a list of assets

it considers exempt property and they notably differ from each other.

5. **Means Test**: A means test is set up by the court to determine whether or not a person is truly bankrupt. It involves evaluating the income, unsecured debt rate, your acclaimed assets and the incurred expenses that have to be paid. Most people who fail this test will not be granted bankruptcy, and others who are, are usually granted a variant. The test becomes necessary after observations are made and confirmed that many people often exploit the policy to live beyond what they could afford.

6. **Lien**: Lien is the legal right that your creditor has to take over some or all of your property because you could not pay up. It is logically given once the earlier deed states that such property should be forfeited the instant payment becomes irregular or defaulted. In other cases, the court may grant such a right to another person's property.

7. **Liquidation**: Liquidation is the condition when the resources of a man are sold after his debts to clear off his old loans. The resources are sold to get "liquids", also known as "cash" which may then be used to pay off the creditors.

8. **Trustee**: A trustee is a person, company or organization which the court appoints to oversee the execution of the debt-paying process. Sometimes, plans are drawn out and funds are scheduled. It is the job of the credit trustee to ensure that all of the loans are paid as tabled out in court. He also serves as the intermediary in cases where assets have to be sold and the liquid generated is shared between every creditor according to the percentage allocated by the court.

At that point, you will need a bankruptcy attorney. You have a slightly rigorous procedure that would be made easier if you have an attorney. Besides, bankruptcy is granted by the court. You have to clearly show that you cannot afford to pay your loans by presenting some files, meeting certain requirements and endorsing some documents. Another thing you should remember is that you can't listen to stories. No two bankruptcy cases are exactly the same. So, everyone has slightly different stories and what has happened to one may never happen to you.

On another note, you would be wondering if you can declare bankruptcy despite having cars or a house. Of course, you can. Cars aren't cash, and you didn't get them when you had no money, so it is possible to have those and still declare bankruptcy. It is only possible that you lose some of your resources, which is contrary to what most people believe. A random person thinks all of your assets have to be sold the instant you declare bankruptcy. Your creditors have to be paid at the end of the day and you still have resources that could be liquidated. But that's not how it works, certain resources will not be lost during bankruptcy, they mostly include resources which you use for work. For example, tools, machines, and their kinds, cars and basic household items like cutleries, furniture, etc. It is also possible to retain your house but you will definitely forfeit resources like pieces of jewelry, tangible investments and so on. The total number of resources that can't be forfeited is determined by the state involved. Each state speculates what qualifies as forfeitable or not.

It is necessary to add that bankruptcy may absolve you of many loans, but that would not include the following. You are required to find some way and pay their full charges:

a. **Court-ordered Child Support**: If you have been ordered by the court to pay something for your child support after divorce, nobody/nothing will waive that money for you, not even bankruptcy.
b. **Court-ordered Alimony:** Alimony is a payment you make to a person pending or after divorce with them. You could stop it if you had started on an informal note, or out of concern for them. But if you have it backed by the court, it becomes legal, binding, and mandatory for you to pay it irrespective of your circumstances. You can only waive this by filing an appeal to the court which is entirely outside bankruptcy.
c. **Government Fines or Court fines**: If you have been slammed with some fine on something you did, whether by the court or a government agency, you are stuck in that too. It is practically impossible to avoid paying that amount no matter your situation.
d. **Reaffirmed Debts**: If you have recently reaffirmed an asset, you are expected to be responsible for it in some way. The court will not hear cases or appeals on how it could be lenient with your reaffirmed debt payment. You are handed a policy and you cannot waive off any of its terms by declaring bankruptcy.
e. **Student Loans**: Well, this isn't usually overlooked by anyone too. It is seen as some investment you definitely benefit from and therefore cannot be waived.

Besides these, the court may deem a few other charges mandatory and you must have some way to pay it back. Usually, this is where personal loans on promissory notes come handy. With those, you can clear off a great part of your loans.

You definitely want to know, there are two types of bankruptcy:

- **Chapter 7 Bankruptcy**: Chapter 7 Bankruptcy is the most popular type of bankruptcy. It is what everyone calls straight bankruptcy, perhaps because it is usually the first option. You need to have a minimum of $1000 unsecured loan in order to announce chapter 7 bankruptcy. You are afterward required to permit a bankruptcy trustee appointed by the court to sell off your assets and pay your creditors. The loan is usually cleared at this point, even if your asset sales do not cover the total amount needed. You are required to pass your *means test* to qualify for this type of bankruptcy plan. Usually, this type of plan will reflect on your credit profile for ten years and cannot be filed for again, until a minimum of seven years.

- **Chapter 13 Bankruptcy**: if you do not qualify for chapter 7 bankruptcy plan, perhaps because you failed your means test or your circumstances require something different, this is the nearest alternative you are shown. That is if your application is not turned down. Unlike the former, it reflects on your credit record for ten years and you can file for it in as little as three years after one. Often, you are allowed to keep as many of your assets as you desire with this plan, and you set up a reaffirmed account with the trustee. You are required to pay all or agreed part of your loans within a three to five-year period after which the rest is discharged. This may sound better on your credit record, considering that you fail a regulation due to inevitable circumstances and brought up a new one that you strictly played by. This type is also called reorganizational bankruptcy, and there are smaller models like chapter 11 and chapter 12 bankruptcy plans, which do not apply to everyone.

Factors to Consider before Declaring Bankruptcy
1. Bankruptcy can't be used every time. What if it seems you might need it more soon? You should save it till then.
2. Do your state policies exempt enough of the assets you would love to keep?
3. What type of bankruptcy are you planning to declare?
4. Can you afford the high prices of Bankruptcy attorneys? Usually, it is not less than $1500 anywhere.
5. Any co-signatory to your account will likely be affected.
6. Are there chances of paying sometime soon?
7. It has a drastic effect on your credit record, especially if you have great statistics on your credit report earlier.

Carefully thinking about these factors can help you decide whether you really want to do this or not. But what can bankruptcy do to your credit score?

The Implication of Bankruptcy on Your Credit Profile
a. **It becomes the terrible part of your credit record**: Having a good credit record before going bankrupt can hurt you a lot. You have breathtaking records debt payment till you run bankrupt and the judgment section becomes a part you wish you could chop off. A part of you hopes that your potential creditors will never check the part with the worst impression on your credit record. It is especially simpler if you have always had a poor record.

b. **It Spoils credit score**: Bankruptcy is declared a negative financial situation. The kind of record that reflects and actually weighs down a good percentage of your credit records. An excellent record may be reduced to a quarter or something more drastic. You will only feel the effects less if you declare when your credit score is extremely poor already.

c. **Reduces your chances of a loan**: Bankruptcy is a condition that gives an impression that the bearer might find it difficult if not impossible to pay up his loans if loaned again, after all, he had been in the shoe and he could not wriggle himself out. Therefore, it is a very high and unwarranted risk to grant such loans to individuals like these when there are others with brighter records who seem able to make do with the funds more and yield better turnouts even in difficult circumstances. That's not even the end, if you eventually secure some loan with such performance, it should be plainly stated that if you manage to get a loan, you could have got it at better terms and lower interest rates if you had better grades. A big disadvantage of bankruptcy.

d. **Opening a new account becomes harder**: It doesn't become difficult to maintain a good record in your old profile alone, it becomes extra hard, though not impossible, to create a new credit account. Credit unions will be plainly reluctant and slow in your request. A situation you wouldn't witness if this hadn't breached.

But among other things, you need to calm your nerves and understand that you can pick your pieces together again. You can rebuild your old and tarnished record to a stronger, impressive and intimidating profile again. Even before the stipulated 8-10years that your bankruptcy can be removed from your profile. As long as you are consistent in your new debts payments and you abide by the regulations strictly. Generally, the different ways you can fix your credit will be discussed in the next chapter.

Chapter Summary

If you are considering filing bankruptcy, there are several factors to put into consideration before doing so. This chapter enlightens you on the types of bankruptcy, its implications on your credit profile, what you stand to gain if you go bankrupt, and every other thing you should know before declaring yourself bankrupt.

CHAPTER NINE
SIMPLE STRATEGIES TO FIX YOUR CREDIT

Fixing your credit is possible, and not as difficult as you have been made to believe. No matter how bad your credit score seems, the ways to magically boost it are, in fact, very simple and practical. Contrary to common myths that a credit score may become so poor that it cannot be fixed, no credit score cannot be fixed. Whenever you find the need to fix one, apply the following strategies:

1. **Hire an expert**: The reason you can manage your company is that you are quite intelligent, and in some way, everyone is. But no matter how good you are, it is always nice to have opinions of an expert in technical cases like this. You have definitely learned lessons as your credit score drastically falls and you struggle to get it up. It isn't a bad idea to hear a couple of incisive words from a colossus. They would help with your budget, plans, financial decisions and so forth. Services like these are sometimes charged and are sometimes free, depending on the motive of the organization or individual you approach. You may hire a credit or financial counselor, an economist, or a bankruptcy attorney, among other specialists.

2. **Work on your history**: Since you have some history to start with and you are starting over, it is always a good idea to review your history. You should find out what you did wrong in each case, what was right and should have been enforced in your transactions. Terms that would be convenient for your business. Policies you can conveniently subscribe to and those you shouldn't ever consider no matter how juicy they seem. You should be on the lookout for errors you didn't note as well, who

charged exorbitantly, whom you can bank on for further business deals and so on.

3. **Be updated on your credit score**: It is a new season and you want to enjoy all the blessings it brings, shutting your eyes, hard as you can, on the other side. One of the ways you can do this is to start monitoring your credit report so it doesn't ever go bad again. No matter how bad it seems already, you are bound to get the best out of it the moment you are always updated with your credit scores and your credit report in general. You have to think about the position of your credit and make informed decisions in your finances every time. Gradually, you can boost your credit scores this way. Besides, you need to keep your eyes on the credit report and your credit bureaus. You deserve a spick-and-span record this time and you shouldn't avoid lapses that can ruin that. So, be updated on your credit information and consider that every time you make financial decisions.

4. **Do not close your old accounts**: Whether your accounts have become delinquent or got to a point you don't want to associate with them, it is always recommended that you still keep them open in some way. Keeping accounts open can serve as an advantage in further credit transactions where they could prove your experience with loans. If you must close an account, however, be sure there is no debt or balance to be covered in it as that can be a big minus to your new account. In fact, it is highly recommended that you avoid creating new credit records at this point.

5. **Reach out to your creditors**: Now this is interesting. A lot of people do not see the need to reach their creditors after their

loans have been activated. Especially if they can afford the charges and there seems no reason to be in touch. But that's not right. It is not always the case that you can pay your monthly dues. Sometimes, you may have huge plans or investments that can't wait till the coming month and your best way to hit this is your monthly debt. If you are in touch with them, establishing firmly that you appreciate their business interaction and you do not mind relating with them beyond the current contract, you will be glad you did. You can count on them at such moments to be lenient and find some way to ensure your credit score is not affected. In fact, a lot of business transactions are conducted on the grounds of the good relationship between the key figures in the business.

6. **Be patient**: your credit score didn't deteriorate in hours; you should expect attempts to rebuild it to take some time too. The different steps you take will not yield many positive results immediately, certainly not as much as you'd like. But it's no reason to despair. It is certainly possible to build it again and it will happen if you are consistent. Do not mind how long the process seems, it always works for those who are consistent. As Harry Hans of *Financial times* would say.

7. **Avoid unnecessary credits:** You surely remember that the federal court on Bankruptcy declared in 2013 that over 70% of unsecured debts are incurred on purchases that could be avoided. You don't want to add a penny to that percentage. It is why you should avoid purchasing items that do not appear in your budget. You should also limit the rate at which you explore markets and rake home some niceties, courtesy of your credit

card. You can hit a nice score again, if you take those tips. None of these is a particularly new principle. They are all simple and practical. Ensure you keep them at heart.

Chapter Summary

This final chapter provides you with viable tested and trusted strategies that could help you build your credit score.

CONCLUSION

MISTAKES TO AVOID DURING CREDIT REPAIR

So far in this wonderful exposition, I have unveiled the core truths about credit and creditworthiness and we have discussed the most vital strategies by which you can repair your credit and boost your credit score from bad to excellent all by yourself. However, it is important not to get so carried away in your desperation to repair your credit that you begin to indulge in the most common errors which may ultimately sabotage your efforts. As a takeaway package, I present to you some of the most salient mistakes to watch against as you repair your credit. From my encounter with people in your shoes who have one difficulty or the other with their credit history, these mistakes are both common and subtle. As a matter of fact, some of them seem to be solutions or hacks in credit repair but they ultimately undo your efforts. Get your highlighter ready!

Failure to Check Credit Reports

This is perhaps the most foundational problem in credit repair. It stems from stark ignorance or mere recklessness or a poor finance-related habit or the intentional refusal to face the facts of your credit status. Well, the truth is that the refusal to own up to your credit mess doesn't take it away. The reality will come haunting you the moment you step into a bank to request loan or you need to apply for a new job and the employer requests it! Regularly checking your credit report keeps you updated with your credit status and helps you identify problem areas to thrash out. It also keeps you abreast with the specific areas where your report is being negatively affected, what information to address or dispute, and what part of your financial involvements to focus on. As far as credit is concerned, the more you know, the better for your credit status. Mores so, bear in mind that it is a great disservice to yourself to wait till a financial firm or employer requests your credit reports before you check them up yourself. There are several known online platforms to check your reports. A typical example is the Federal Trade Commission Free Credits Report page.

Failure to Pay Down Debt Quickly

What many do not realize is that paying off your debts, and quickly too, is one of the most assured ways to remedy your bad credit. The way out is to offset your debts in small regular bits. Staying true to a particular pattern of debt clearance greatly improves your credit score. Take down credits seriously, especially the credit cards that are close to being maxed out. Another similarly significant approach is to pay your installment loans such as student loans and auto loans, depending on which ones apply to you. Constantly reducing your loans and debts does not only improve your credit score but sells you as a dependable and responsible client to future employers, loan firms, banks and other finance-related organizations.

Improper or No Documentation

Documentation is highly essential to arriving at an awesome credit score. It is wrong to fail to take documentation of every financial activity you engage in. Your spending history is one of the factors put into consideration by credit bureaus to calculate your credit score. This explains why you should never agree to an oral agreement; however flimsy it seems. All payments should be backed with paperwork or at least receipts. In as much as there is a financial commitment attached to it, ensure you have it properly documented. Your documented payments and financial activities come in handy when or if you have a reason to dispute a report later in the future. Bureaus do not work with oral agreements, so if you have been offsetting a debt or repaying a loan, for example, ensure it is well documented.

Excessive Disputes

Mistakes are inevitable in credit reports. Most times, they are the consequences of insufficient information, which may be caused by improper documentation as mentioned above. When you notice an error in your report, it is only normal to react by filing a dispute. In an earlier chapter of this book, I already discussed the benefits of filing disputes, and how to write an effective dispute letter. However, filing excessive disputes will do quite the opposite to your credit reports. More so, it is wrong to dispute the entire report. You should dispute only information you are sure about, and you have adequate backup or evidence to prove.

Filing for Bankruptcy

Filing for bankruptcy is a rather delicate credit repair approach you should use with caution because it never really helps your credit. Of course, it temporarily liberates you from the debt load, and makes you focus on other productive financial commitments, you must bear in mind that bankruptcy never really works without affecting your future creditworthiness. It leaves a taint on your credit. File for bankruptcy today, and it remains glued to your credit history for at least seven to ten years, thereby holding the likelihood of impeding a future loan.

Transferring Credit Card Balances

Sometimes, credit repair experts and companies suggest transferring credit balances from card to card as am credit repair technique but this is always not a good idea. It does not reduce nor take away the amount of debts you owe. More so, you will still have to sacrifice your interests because most times, the transfer fees overshadow whatever interests you might get. Some persons do this because they want to close the other credit cards and consolidate their debts onto one single credit card. In the end, you lose more than you gain. You sacrifice the credit history you have so far garnered on the credit cards you wish to close.

Canceling Credit Card Accounts

Is this really a good idea? Maybe not! You can never increase your credit score by closing your credit cards. The truth about your credit report, as you have learned so far, is that there are so many factors in place. Closing a credit card account with many bad records such as debts, late payments, and so on, seems to be able to boost your credit score, but on the contrary, that is not so. This is because the length of your credit history is one of the major factors that inputs your credit report. Closing an account does nothing but to reduce the length of your credit card history, thereby making you lose some points in that regard. The most vital way out is to keep the accounts and reduce the low payments on them.

Getting Back into Bad Debts

Bad debts are quick ways to lose points on your credit score. It is normal and even recommended to secure a loan for a business activity that will yield much more than the loan and the interests put together. That is a good debt, but anything contrary is a bad debt. Bad debts leave you frustrated and leave your credit score affected. After clearing off a debt, many individuals and small corporations often go back into debts in a bid to raise enough funds for their business activities and engagements. While this isn't an entirely bad idea, what is bad about it is the nature of loans they have acquired and the terms involved, which often results in debts that are difficult to pay. Unfortunately, too many bad debts sabotage your efforts to build both your business and your credit score.

Hiring a Shady Credit Repair Company

Although hiring a credit repair company or expert isn't a bad idea for persons who do not have the expertise or patience to undertake the process involved in repairing or fixing a bad credit score, it comes with its own disadvantages and cost. Most credit repair companies, in a bid to impress their clients, blindly dispute credit reports. This is often the first step towards failure. At the end of the day, many positive information is removed from the client's records. Another major downside to hiring credit repair companies is the cost involved. According to Credit Karma, service charges of such companies range from about $50 to $150 on a monthly basis for services you could render yourself with a few tips and patience.

Being impatient

Credit fixing is no miracle. It requires diligence and patience. You need to stay committed to the ideas over time in order to get positive outcome. The attitude towards your credit repair will result in slow but certain outcome which will eventually culminate over the years, depending on the extent of damage already done to your credit. With the right DIY tips applied well, you are on your way to a credit score of over 720.

www.ingramcontent.com/pod-product-compliance
Lightning Source LLC
Chambersburg PA
CBHW070423220526
45466CB00004B/1516